T0311738

Cambridge Elements ☰

Elements in England in the Early Medieval World
edited by
Megan Cavell
University of Birmingham
Rory Naismith
University of Cambridge
Winfried Rudolf
University of Göttingen
Emily V. Thornbury
Yale University

ART AND THE FORMATION OF EARLY MEDIEVAL ENGLAND

Catherine E. Karkov
University of Leeds

CAMBRIDGE
UNIVERSITY PRESS

CAMBRIDGE
UNIVERSITY PRESS

University Printing House, Cambridge CB2 8BS, United Kingdom

One Liberty Plaza, 20th Floor, New York, NY 10006, USA

477 Williamstown Road, Port Melbourne, VIC 3207, Australia

314–321, 3rd Floor, Plot 3, Splendor Forum, Jasola District Centre,
New Delhi – 110025, India

103 Penang Road, #05–06/07, Visioncrest Commercial, Singapore 238467

Cambridge University Press is part of the University of Cambridge.

It furthers the University's mission by disseminating knowledge in the pursuit of
education, learning, and research at the highest international levels of excellence.

www.cambridge.org
Information on this title: www.cambridge.org/9781108931977
DOI: 10.1017/9781108942935

First published 2022

A catalogue record for this publication is available from the British Library.

ISBN 978-1-108-93197-7 Paperback
ISSN 2632-203X (online)
ISSN 2632-2021 (print)

Art and the Formation of Early Medieval England

Elements in England in the Early Medieval World

DOI: 10.1017/9781108942935
First published online: February 2022

Catherine E. Karkov
University of Leeds

Author for correspondence: Catherine E. Karkov, c.e.karkov@leeds.ac.uk

Abstract: This Element covers the art produced in early medieval England from the departure of the Romans to the early twelfth century, an art that shows the input of multi-ethnic artists, patrons, and influences as it develops over the centuries. Art in early medieval England is an art of migrants and colonisers, and the Element considers the ways in which it was defined and developed by the different groups that travelled to or settled on the island. It also explores some of the key forms and images that define the art of the period and the role of both material and artist/patron in their creation. Art is an expression of identity, whether individual, regional, national, religious, or institutional, and this Element sheds light on the way art in early medieval England was and continues to be used to define particular identities, including that of the island on which it was produced.

Keywords: materiality, migration, postcolonial, early medieval England, early medieval art

ISBNs: 9781108931977 (PB), 9781108942935 (OC)
ISSNs: 2632-203X (online), 2632-2021 (print)

Contents

1 Migrants and Colonisers

This Element is about the art of the period roughly 500–1100 CE, but there was no entity recognised as 'England' until the tenth century, hence this Element's title *Art and the Formation of Early Medieval England*. Before England there was Britannia (the Roman name for the island), inhabited by the multiple Brittonic peoples who would eventually become the Scots, the Welsh, and the Cornish. All of them had arrived on the island long before the Romans, and others continued to arrive during and after the Roman occupation. This brief summary highlights the fact that, culturally and ethnically, the island was a diverse place, and so all art on the island is ultimately the work of migrants and colonisers. The art of pre-Roman Britannia is abstract, curvilinear, and largely non-representational, and it displays a love of pattern, movement, and colour. The Romans defined it as 'barbaric', meaning simply that it was non-Roman, but it was distinctly different from the Roman interest in naturalistic and figural forms, pictorial narrative, and monumentality. With the arrival of the Romans a hybrid art developed, especially in areas of close cultural contact such as the Hadrian's Wall corridor. The hybridity of form and image this produced continued to be a rich source of inspiration for artists into the eighth century and, in some places, beyond. The early-eighth-century Lindisfarne Gospels (London, BL, Cotton MS Nero D.iv) is a work in which we see Roman influence in, for example, the portraits of the evangelists seated at their desks, with Brittonic influence in the dynamic abstract patterns of the incipit pages to the individual gospels.[1]

The Brittonic peoples were migrants, settling discrete areas of the island and living alongside each other sometimes in peace and sometimes in conflict. The Romans, however, were colonisers intent on claiming the island, or at least as much of it as they could manage to hold on to, by military strength. They met with considerable resistance, but, in becoming part of the Roman Empire, the island became part of a much larger political and cultural order that stretched across Europe and into areas of the Middle East and Africa. It is here that we can locate the beginnings of what would become England in the early medieval world. Not only was the island now linked to vast trading networks, but the Roman presence included individuals from other Roman provinces, at least some of whom stayed on after the departure of Roman troops in the early fifth century.[2] For example, 11 per cent of the bodies at the Trentholme Drive, York, cemetery are of likely African ancestry.[3] Many sites were abandoned when the

---

[1] See www.bl.uk/manuscripts/FullDisplay.aspx?index=14&ref=Cotton_MS_Nero_D_IV.
[2] See further Gowland, 'Embodied Identities'.
[3] Montgomery Ramírez, 'Colonial Representations', 5.

Romans withdrew, others were gradually deserted, and still others remained inhabited but by different population groups who converted them to different functions. An elaborate floor mosaic in the Roman villa at Chedworth (Cotswolds) dated 424–544 CE shows a decline in artistic standards from fourth-century mosaics but also the continuation of an elite and very Roman style of life.[4] The Roman city of Wroxeter (Shropshire) doesn't preserve such lavish artworks but is thought to have remained inhabited and functioned as a town into at least the late fifth century, while the Roman fort at Birdoswald (Cumbria) was partially demolished and its walls used to enclose a new settlement with new wooden buildings in the fifth century.[5] There was also significant continuity in the use of farmland.[6]

Interpretation of archaeological evidence for the decades after the Roman departure is fraught with disagreement and uncertainty, but it is indisputable that, whether as raiders, settlers, or colonisers, groups of people from the coastal areas across the North Sea arrived on the island during the fifth and sixth centuries. Gildas (c.500–c.570) described them as barbarians, wolves, and dogs.[7] Bede, whose *Ecclesiastical History of the English People* created an enduring image of the early English as a people,[8] names them as the Angles, Saxons, and Jutes, although he was writing centuries after their arrival. Whatever the reality on the ground, by the eighth century the narrative had come to be one of violent conquest, and the Britons were eventually confined to Wales, and the Scots and Picts to areas north of Hadrian's Wall. Archaeological evidence indicates that there was also much interaction, cooperation, and assimilation between all these peoples. The evolution of pottery designs in the Nene Valley, for instance, suggests both a gradual adoption and production of new designs by British artists.[9] Colonisation is a long process, not a single event or even a series of events, and it is a process that is not limited to violence against the colonised.[10] Ultimately, it was the Angles, Saxons, and Jutes, all of whom spoke Germanic rather than Brittonic languages, who would form the early English kingdoms which during the tenth century were brought together under a single king to become England. Traditionally known as the 'Anglo-Saxons', a term now being abandoned due to its racist implications, their art was

---

[4] Morris, 'Stunning Dark Age Mosaic'.

[5] For Wroxeter: Barker et al., *Baths-Basilica Wroxeter*. For Birdoswald: Wilmott, *Birdoswald*. See more generally: Gerrard, *Ruin of Britain*.

[6] Oosthuizen, *Emergence of the English*, 106–19.   [7] Winterbottom, *Ruin of Britain*, 26, 97.

[8] See, for example, Story, Ormrod, and Tyler, 'Framing Migration', 1–3.

[9] Oosthuizen, *Emergence of the English*, 33–4.

[10] Wolfe, 'Settler Colonialism'. For example, the British kingdom of Rheged became part of Anglian Northumbria through intermarriage, conversion, baptism, and possibly the erection of stone monuments carved in an Anglian style (Orton and Wood with Lees, *Fragments of History*, 121–5).

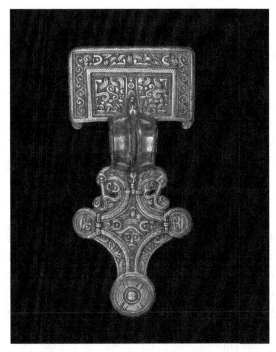

Figure 1 Chessell Down brooch, British
Museum. © The Trustees of the British Museum.

influenced by contact with the Roman world but characterised by animal and
abstract ornament and portability, a combination exemplified by a fifth-century
buckle from Mucking, Essex.[11] This is the point at which the art of early
medieval England can truly be said to begin.

Surviving art of the sixth and seventh centuries consists mostly of portable
metalwork objects such as jewellery, coins, weapons, and items of personal
dress. The focus on portable rather than more monumental forms of art likely
reflects the unsettled nature of kingdoms in formation, with their shifting
borders and political and religious centres. Most of this metalwork comes
from graves, such as the early-sixth-century square-headed brooch from
a woman's grave at Chessell Down, Isle of Wight (Figure 1) and the early-
sixth-century drinking horn mounts from a 'princely burial' at Taplow,
Buckinghamshire.[12] Both are silver-gilt, and both are decorated with Style
I animal ornament. The motifs of Style I had their origins in fifth-century
Scandinavia, but the chip-carving technique used on these pieces comes from

---

[11] See www.britishmuseum.org/collection/object/H_1970–0406-26-b.
[12] See www.britishmuseum.org/collection/object/H_1883–1214-20.

Roman art. The term chip-carving (*kerbschnitt*) refers to the faceted surfaces of the pieces that look as if they had been chipped away, with a chisel. Style I reached south-eastern England in the late fifth century and flourished during the first half of the sixth. The brooch's fragmented and highly stylised animals and masks are typical of the style. Animals and humans are reduced to just one or two body parts, as can be seen in the three faces that stare out from the brooch's foot-plate. At the centre of the foot-plate is a double bird-headed creature (or two bird heads flanking a helmeted head). Two dots form its eyes and the curving C-shapes suggest its heads, from which tiny curving beaks project. There are four abstract creatures facing away from each other and towards the circular lobes of the foot-plate in the lower borders outside the central lozenge. Above the foot-plate are two downturned animal heads with open mouths, each side of which ends in a tiny head. Above them, the bow of the brooch ends in a relief mask like an arching human-headed serpent. It is nose-to-nose with another stylised animal. Two more stylised animals crawl away from each other in the upper border of the head-plate; their leg-like limbs are visible to either side of its centre and their heads and curving beaks near its edges. They appear to crawl towards the scrolling patterns that fill the side borders. Each of the two halves of the head-plate's central panel is filled with pairs of human–animal hybrids separated by S-shaped scrolls. Their limbs are visible in the outer corners of the panel's upper edge and to either side of the relief mask that divides it. Small dots form their eyes.

The ornament's meaning is uncertain though it is assumed to be apotro-paic, meaning that it was designed to protect the wearer from danger or evil. The human–animal hybrids and the confrontations between creatures might represent supernatural beings and a battle (or perhaps harmony) between different or opposing forces. The frontal face that looks out from beneath the bird heads in the foot-plate could represent Woden with his two ravens.[13]

The brooch comes from a woman's grave, as do most Style I objects, though not the most luxurious objects. It is an item of jewellery, with its ornament considered protective for the wearer, as noted. Early medieval English women are often interpreted as passive displays of a husband or family's wealth and power rather than powerful or aggressive in their own right, but, as with the status of migrants, this is being rethought. Queens and elite women did pursue political roles and fight for favoured causes or beliefs. Ælfflæd, Abbess of Whitby (654–714), maintained an active interest in Northumbrian court life. Æthelthryth of Ely (c.636–79) defied her royal

---

[13] Webster, *Anglo-Saxon Art*, 17.

husband to become a nun and donated the land for Hexham Abbey to Bishop Wilfrid, while her successor as queen, Iurminburh, maintained a highly political feud with Wilfrid.

Style I on male-associated objects, on the other hand, is considered symbolic of 'male warrior status'.[14] The Taplow drinking horn with the Style I mounts around its rim is a prime example. Drinking horns were elite items, and the mounts, older than the early-seventh-century grave in which they were found, were probably heirlooms, possibly representing lineage or heritage. The fragmented tangled forms in the triangular fields and flanking the relief masks in the panels surrounding the rim are examples of the 'helmet and hand' motif. The figures' hands are raised in front of their faces, and their heads are covered by a curving 'helmet'. It is possible that this latter detail is not a helmet at all but some other form of headdress or simply an extension of the linear design crowning the heads of the human forms on the Chessell Down brooch. The same type of head is found on a variety of objects, including brooches, for which a military context is not evident. That does not mean to say that the occupant of the Taplow princely burial was not a warrior. The issue is the language we use and the way it has served to create an image of a period defined by only two clearly distinguished gender possibilities – male and female – with normalised male violence and female passivity or servility as its distinguishing features. This, in addition to its casting as the origin of a people (rather than just a political geography),[15] has made it easy for white supremacists and nationalist groups to appropriate it to their causes. What is rarely mentioned about the Taplow burial is that it also contained a two-handled Coptic bowl with a scalloped rim and open-work decoration above the foot that came from the eastern Mediterranean.[16] It is one of a number of objects produced in the eastern Mediterranean, Africa, or India demonstrating that, early on, the people of England had a sense of themselves as part of a much larger and more diverse world. The grave-goods from the contemporary Mound 1 Sutton Hoo burial display similarly wide connections with jewellery decorated with garnets originating in India or Sri Lanka, Merovingian coins, silver spoons and bowls from Byzantium or the eastern Mediterranean, textile fragments woven using a Syrian technique, Scandinavian-influenced weaponry, and shoulder clasps (or fasteners for a chest protector) possibly made by a Byzantine-trained

---

[14] Webster, *Anglo-Saxon Art*, 60; Mittman and MacCormack, 'Rebuilding'.

[15] For example, the introductory essay of the catalogue for *The Making of England* begins, 'The Anglo-Saxons, whose artistic, technological and cultural achievements in the seventh, eighth, and ninth centuries are displayed in this exhibition, were the true ancestors of the English today'; Brooks, 'Historical Introduction', 9.

[16] See www.britishmuseum.org/collection/object/H_1883-1214-8.

goldsmith.[17] However, it is generally the regalia and military gear that garner the most scholarly and popular attention.[18]

The great gold belt buckle from Mound 1 displays Style II decoration, which became popular in England in the late sixth century.[19] Style II is characterised by elongated ribbon-bodied animal ornament with the knotted or interlaced animals remaining whole, coherent bodies and by the disappearance of human mask motifs. The front-plate of the buckle is decorated with twelve symmetrically paired interlaced creatures and a single thirteenth animal between the jaws of two beasts at one end.

The Christian church was another early incomer to the island. Christianity was practised during the Roman occupation but only on a limited scale. The Romans left no major Christian centres that survived the century or so after their withdrawal. Individual monastic centres were established during the fifth and sixth centuries, especially in the north and west. Gildas is thought to have received his monastic education in South Wales, possibly at Cor Tewdws, under Illtud, who came to Britain from northern France. Columba came from Ireland to found Iona in 563, and Augustine arrived in Kent from Rome in 597, possibly with the Italian-made St Augustine's Gospels (C.C. C.C., MS 286). The remains of a fifth- or sixth-century church and fragments of a fifth-century lead chalice – decorated with images that include crosses, angels, ships, fish, and a whale and inscribed with letters in Greek, Latin, and possibly Ogham – from the Roman fort of Vindolanda on Hadrian's Wall have provided evidence of a significant ecclesiastical site in northern England in the immediate post-Roman period.[20] Monks, teachers, and craftspeople from across Europe and Ireland were members of these early monastic communities, which must have been diverse and multilingual places. Writing towards the end of the ninth century, King Alfred lamented the fact that both learning and the knowledge of multiple languages that had flourished during the age of Bede had disappeared by his own day – although some knowledge of Latin, the universal language of the western church, remained.[21]

The c.600 grave of a teenage girl whose DNA showed her to be of sub-Saharan West African descent in Kent indicates that migrants from that area had arrived in Britain at an early date; however, very little else can be said about how the girl's ancestor came to be here, and a full report on the grave has yet to be published.[22] The remains of Black men and women living in England in the late

---

[17] Adams, 'Sutton Hoo Shoulder Clasps'. [18] Allfrey, 'Sutton Hoo in Public'.

[19] See www.britishmuseum.org/collection/object/H_1939-1010-1.

[20] Alberge, 'Hadrian's Wall Dig'.

[21] Schreiber, *King Alfred's Old English Translation*, 191–9. [22] Hines, 'Future of the Past'.

Saxon period have also been recovered from St Benet's (York), North Elmham (Norfolk), and Fairford (Gloucestershire).[23] It is possible that the number of migrants from Africa or of African descent present on the island in the early medieval period was significant.[24] Research tends to focus on the well-known individuals, sites, and stories, while other less clearly documented stories are lost. At the end of the seventh century, one such well-known individual, Theodore, a Byzantine Greek from Tarsus in the eastern Mediterranean, became archbishop of Canterbury. He was accompanied by Hadrian from Cyrenia in Libya, a refugee from the Arab invasion of North Africa, who became abbot of the monastery of St Peter's (later St Augustine's) in Canterbury.[25] The two certainly also brought books and other objects with them, although none now survives. It is likely that some Byzantine manuscripts came north and west with them, given the focus on Greek language and learning in their educational reforms – perhaps icons too, as they are credited with introducing some eastern saints to the island. They established an important school of Greek and Latin learning at Canterbury, introducing knowledge of the saints and the eastern church, the study of poetry and music, and perhaps also knowledge of Coptic art. Details of the history and education of both Theodore and Hadrian are few, but Theodore was familiar with the art and architecture of Constantinople and also of Rome, where he was a monk for a number of years.[26] Hadrian, from Greek-speaking North Africa, was also familiar with Byzantine art and learning along with Egyptian culture, bringing this knowledge to the monastery near Naples that was his home before England. He had also been a confidant of both the pope and the Byzantine emperor,[27] and thus he was familiar with the luxury art of both worlds.

The art and/or artists that accompanied Theodore and Hadrian to England remain unknown, but a sustained interest in the Greek-speaking world from which the two men came is evident in the eighth century, the period in which we would expect their influence on education and monastic culture to become broadly apparent. Oxford, Bodleian Library, MS Douce 140 contains a mid-eighth-century copy of Primasius's *Commentarius in Apocalypsin*. Primasius wrote his Latin commentary in what is now Sousse, Tunisia, in the middle of the sixth century, at which time the city was part of the Byzantine Empire. It is a rare text, although Bede consulted a version of it for his own *Commentary on the*

---

[23] Montgomery Ramírez, 'Colonial Representations', 4–6.

[24] Green, 'Evidence for African Migrants in Britain'.

[25] See further Rambaran-Olm and Wade, *Race in Early Medieval England*; Rambaran-Olm, 'Wrinkle in Medieval Time'.

[26] Bischoff and Lapidge, *Biblical Commentaries*, 42, 60.

[27] Bischoff and Lapidge, *Biblical Commentaries*, 13.

Apocalypse, and the Oxford manuscript is written in an unusual script that seems to copy a continental or African exemplar.[28] The influence of Theodore and Hadrian on art takes a backseat to their influence on learning and liturgy, but it can be seen in the art produced by the generation that would have studied under them. Early-eighth-century manuscripts from southern England display a lavishness, classicising style, and use of gold and silver that is broadly Roman or Mediterranean but has similarities with the seventh-century Byzantine art with which Theodore and Hadrian were familiar. Both the 725–50 Vespasian Psalter (London, BL, Cotton MS Vespasian A.i) and the mid-eighth-century Codex Aureus (Stockholm, Kungliga Biblioteket, MS A.135) have been attributed to Canterbury – the former to St Augustine's – but it is not necessary for them to have been made in Canterbury for them to show its influence.

The Vespasian Psalter, the earliest surviving illuminated Southumbrian manuscript, boasts two of the earliest historiated initials, initials that contain figures or abbreviated narrative scenes that relate directly to the text they introduce. The initial introducing Psalm 26 (fol. 31r) depicts David and Jonathan holding spears and clasping hands, while the initial to Psalm 52 (fol. 53r) depicts David rescuing the lamb from the lion.[29] The scribe-artist has been described as 'a master who drew upon Italo-Byzantine, "oriental", Frankish and Hiberno-Saxon' sources.[30] Its model may have been a sixth-century Byzantine psalter brought north by Theodore, as it makes lavish use of gold and silver, materials particularly, though not exclusively, associated with Byzantine manuscripts.[31] The foliate designs flanking the arch above David's head in the miniature of David composing the psalms (fol. 30v) and the columns that support the arch have similarities with the carved capitals, impost blocks, and inlaid columns of churches like St Polyeuktos, Constantinople (c.520), while the painterly modelling of elements of the bodies and draperies of the figures combined with their thick dark contour lines can be compared with those of sixth-century Coptic icons. The figure style and naturalistic movements of the figures – David is playing the strings of his lyre with realistic hand positions – are unprecedented in northern manuscript illumination. David's ankles show through the folds of his robe in a suggestion of transparent cloth rare in early medieval England. Both these details and the energetic poses of the dancers before him have sources in manuscripts such as the sixth-century Vienna Genesis probably produced in Syria (Vienna, Österreichische Nationalbibliothek, cod. Theol. Gr. 31). The trumpet-scrolls

---

[28] Breay and Story, *Anglo-Saxon Kingdoms*, 132.

[29] A complete facsimile of the manuscript is available: www.bl.uk/manuscripts/FullDisplay.aspx?ref=Cotton_MS_Vespasian_A_I.

[30] Webster and Backhouse, *Making of England*, 197.　　[31] Wright, *Vespasian Psalter*.

filling the arch, as well as the animal ornament and dot stippling seen on other pages of the manuscript, are typical of earlier Insular art. The script is primarily uncials, a luxury script associated with Roman manuscripts. It is a truly cosmopolitan style suited to the linguistic and cultural diversity of Theodore and Hadrian's Canterbury.

The Codex Aureus is close in style to the Vespasian Psalter but more lavish in its appearance and materials.[32] It consists of alternating plain vellum and purple stained pages, the latter reminiscent of the imperial manuscripts of Rome and Constantinople. In Byzantium the colour purple was reserved for the imperial court. The text is written in gold, silver, white, and coloured inks. Different inks have been used to pick out letters and words creating visual interest and, in some instances, working cruciform patterns into the text. Crosses and other geometric shapes have also been used to frame areas of text, a textual patterning and display associated with the *carmina figurata* of Constantine's court poet Porphyrius. A mid-eighth-century letter from the bishop of Mainz complains that a copy of Porphyrius's work had been borrowed but not returned by Cuthbert, archbishop of Canterbury, so this could have been the model for the Codex Aureus. Only two evangelist portraits, Matthew and John, survive, both painted on plain vellum versos facing purple incipit pages. The opening of John's gospel is especially grand, befitting its special status in early England. John (Figure 2) is shown frontally displaying his open book. It's possible that the first words of his gospel were to have been written on its open pages, as they are on the scroll held by Matthew on folio 9v. His chair is decorated with vine-scroll, and the columns supporting the arch are painted purple with spiral patterning, a possible reference to the twisted columns surrounding the shrine of St Peter in Rome. His halo and the decorative circles on the curtains are filled with gold. The figure style is like that of the Vespasian Psalter but even more classicising, with a greater suggestion of the bulk of the body beneath the drapery. The ankles again show through the transparent cloth covering them. The shading and highlighting on John's face and arms create a more subtly modelled figure, and even his fingernails have been delicately outlined. On the facing page, the opening words of his gospel are written in display capitals using coloured inks that originally stood out against a gold leaf background panel. These classicising elements are balanced by the canon tables, which are filled with interlace patterns and trumpet spirals derived from Insular art. Several of their arcades are treated as decorative patterns rather than architectural structures, their bases replaced by roundels which in three cases (folios 6r–7r) are linked together by ornamental bands hanging like chains from the roundels.

---

[32] See https://archive.org/details/urn-nbn-se-kb-digark-4890092.

Figure 2 John the Evangelist, Stockholm Codex Aureus, Stockholm, Kungliga
Biblioteket, MS A.135, fol. 150v. Wikimedia Commons/CC-SA-1.0.

The Codex Aureus is famous for its chi-rho page (Figure 3), which celebrates
the incarnation of Christ and receives special attention in English and Irish
manuscripts. In this manuscript the text, aside from the first line, is written in
alternating registers of gold capitals against a plain vellum background and
capitals in coloured ink against a gold background. In the first line, the X of
Christ's monogram is a dynamic curving shape with two terminals ending in
golden beast heads that set the monogram off from the rest of the line. The arms
of the X extend beyond the frame, suggesting the uncontainable nature of
Christ. The body of the X and the background of the panel to the right are filled

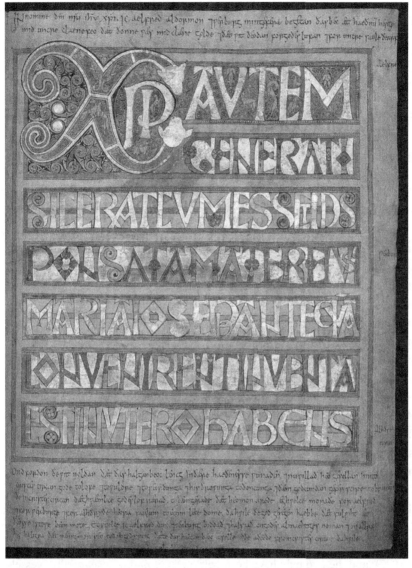

Figure 3 Chi-rho page, Stockholm Codex Aureus, Stockholm, Kungliga Biblioteket, MS A.135, fol. 11r. Wikimedia Commons/public domain.

with interlace containing animals and tiny humans in a Mercian style and indicative of the life residing in Christ and his church. To the left and beneath the X are trumpet spiral and trefoil patterns much like those that fill the columns of the canon tables. Together the designs of this single line represent the movement of Christ from the cosmos into his incarnation. However, the page is probably best known for the marginal note added by a ninth-century

Canterbury scribe recording the book's theft and recovery. It states that Ealdorman Ælfred, his wife Werberg, and their daughter Alhthryth ransomed the book from the Viking army and gave it to Canterbury in exchange for prayers for their souls.

The Norse raids on early England began in earnest at the end of the eighth century, bringing widespread looting of treasures like the Codex Aureus. The raiders came primarily from the areas of Denmark and Norway, and they began settling in England around the mid-ninth century. Although they never conquered the island, their presence had a profound impact on art, culture, and language, especially in the north, the political centre of the Danelaw. Recent archaeological work has shown that they also brought craftspeople with them from their homelands.[33]

In their new home the Scandinavians became associated with two particular art forms: metalwork and stone sculpture. Manuscripts like the Codex Aureus were taken for their valuable treasure-bindings of gold, silver, enamelwork, and precious stones, which could be removed and melted down, traded, or used as portable wealth and the manuscript pages ransomed back. Hoards from the period provide evidence of the range of material collected. The Vale of York hoard found near Harrogate consisted of 617 coins, sixty-seven pieces of silver including six silver arm-rings, one gold arm-ring, and a mid-ninth-century Carolingian silver-gilt cup.[34] The coins date the hoard to 927–8, meaning it was most probably buried to protect it during the tumultuous events of King Athelstan's reign. All the objects had been packed in a lead box before burial. The gold arm-ring is decorated with two rows of V-shaped punch marks, a technique common in Scandinavian jewellery. One of the silver arm-rings is also decorated with punch marks, and a second is made of thick silver wires twisted around each other, another common type of Scandinavian ornament. The rest of the silver consisted of plain arm-rings, ingots, and hack silver, including a fragment of a penannular brooch decorated with bosses and animal ornament. The cup is a pair with a bowl from the Halton Moor hoard (buried c.1027), and the two may have been heirlooms or part of a set of altar vessels that arrived in England during the ninth century, perhaps as loot, or tribute, or simply as gifts.[35] The ninth-century date of the cup and bowl coincides with a period in which increasing influence from the Carolingian court became apparent in both art and intellectual culture. The coins, however, come from Samarkand, North Africa, northern Russia, and Afghanistan, providing evidence of the extensive trading networks in which the Scandinavians

---

[33] Hadley, 'Archaeology of Migrants', 186–93.   [34] Williams and Ager, *Vale of York Hoard*.
[35] Webster, *Anglo-Saxon Art*, 156.

participated. The hoard's jewellery included broken and intact items from Ireland, Scandinavia, and Russia.

Stone sculpture was not a prominent art form in early Scandinavian cultures, although it was not entirely unknown. It was, however, an important Anglian art form, and the Scandinavians quickly adapted it to their own requirements, developing new forms such as the hogback (a memorial shaped like a longhouse with a curving ridged roof), introducing new motifs and styles, and increasing sculptural production in some areas by a factor of five during the tenth century.[36] The period also saw sculpture produced for secular patrons coming to dominate that produced for ecclesiastical patrons. 'Secular' subject matter may also have increased, although it is often impossible to make a clear distinction between the secular and the sacred. On the tenth-century Leeds Cross, for example, the figure holding a sword and accompanied by a bird in the lowest panel of one of the broad sides (Figure 4) may represent the patron, his image perhaps helping to express personal or dynastic claims to land, status, or local power.[37] Alternatively, he could be someone commemorated by the cross, his position at the base of the shaft echoing that of individuals commemorated on earlier Anglian sculpture, such as the eighth-century Bewcastle Cross.[38] Swords and birds of prey are attributes of elite male status, and the knotwork design beneath his sword may be a sign that he has passed out of this world. Alternatively, he could represent a legendary figure such as Sigurd the dragon slayer or Weland the Smith. Weland escaping imprisonment with his flying machine appears level with this panel on the opposite face of the cross. Although the original cross-head is missing, this was definitely a Christian monument, one of a group of crosses worked with similar motifs. The reasons for the inclusion of polytheistic or legendary figures on this and other monuments of the period are not always clear. They are commonly interpreted as signs of synchronicity – or attempted harmony – between the differing religions and cultures. In such a scenario, the dragon-slayer and ascending smith could represent types of Christ defeating evil and ascending into heaven. On the other hand, such images could as easily be general statements of Scandinavian identity and power within a culture that had come to value ecclesiastical patronage by members of the aristocracy. Difficulties in interpreting the iconographic programme of the Leeds Cross are

---

[36] Bailey, *C.A.S.S.S. 9*, *Cheshire and Lancashire*, 19.

[37] For a full discussion of the cross, see Coatsworth, *C.A.S.S.S. 8*, *Western Yorkshire*, catalogue Leeds 1; https://chacklepie.com/ascorpus/catvol8.php?pageNum_urls=150.

[38] See Bailey and Cramp, *C.A.S.S.S. 2*, *Cumberland, Westmorland and Lancashire North-of-the-Sands*, ch. 7 and catalogue Bewcastle 1; https://chacklepie.com/ascorpus/catvol2.php?pageNum_urls=30.

Figure 4 Leeds Cross, portrait of patron. © Corpus of Anglo-Saxon Stone
Sculpture, photographers K. P. Jukes and D. J. Craig.

made much worse by the fact that it was broken up and used as building
material.

Cnut, king of England (1016–35), Denmark (1018–35), and Norway and
parts of Sweden (1028–35), made England again part of an empire, albeit
a short-lived one. Ælfgyfu/Emma, his queen, was of Norman birth and had
been married previously to the English king Æthelred II. Her mother was
Danish and Normandy was a Scandinavian settlement, although it certainly

remained outside of the areas over which Cnut reigned. At his death the crown eventually went to Edward the Confessor (son of Ælfgyfu/Emma and Æthelred II), who died childless. The ensuing battle for the crown ended in the Norman Conquest of 1066. The turmoil of the eleventh century with its two conquests of 1016 and 1066 has been much studied.[39] Both had a profound impact on the art of England with the introduction of new types of art, such as monumental architectural sculpture and new forms of architecture; new subject matter, such as scenes of the harrowing of hell during the reign of Cnut; and new styles, such as the early Romanesque style of architecture seen in buildings like Durham Cathedral (Figure 5). The art that developed during the eleventh century also presents new problems of interpretation. There is an ambivalence to much eleventh-century art that is no doubt a result of the political turmoil with its financial and sometimes military attacks on religious houses and the difficulty of safely documenting or reacting to the events and often rapid changes that took place.[40] One of the places this can be seen most clearly is Durham, home to the community of St Cuthbert which had finally settled there in 875.

Durham housed the shrine of St Cuthbert, the bones of Bede, and the head of St Oswald, and it was a potential centre of English national resistance. It also enjoyed the patronage of King Malcolm III (Canmore) and Queen Margaret of Scotland. Margaret was the granddaughter of Æthelred II and his first wife, as well as being the daughter of Edward the Exile. She and her brother, Edgar Ætheling (1051–1126), were thus the last surviving direct descendants of the West Saxon royal line. Edgar had in fact been named king in 1066 but had never been crowned. He fled to Scotland in 1068 and – with Scottish, Danish, and English support – led a briefly successful rebellion in the North in 1069. William quashed the rebellion, destroying many pre-Conquest monuments, during what became known as the Harrying of the North. Edgar fled back to Scotland, but the North remained an unstable area for decades. As an assertion of Norman power, Durham Cathedral was placed under the control of ecclesiastics loyal to William, and the cathedral was rebuilt in the new Anglo-Norman (or early Romanesque) style. It is considered amongst the finest examples of the new style to survive.

William of Saint-Calais became prince-bishop of Durham in 1080 and began a building campaign in 1083. The integrated cathedral-castle complex that resulted was representative of the combined religious, political, and military authority exercised by the prince bishops and a statement of Norman dominance that towered over the surrounding landscape. The new cathedral was intended

---

[39] See Ashe and Ward, *Conquests*.

[40] Karkov, 'Conquest and Material Culture'; Karkov 'Reading the Trinity'; Treharne, *Living Through Conquest*.

Figure 5 Durham Cathedral, photo by author.

from the start to be reminiscent of St Peter's, Rome. Its dimensions were based on those of St Peter's, and the chevrons and other designs carved into the piers of the nave recalled the spiral columns surrounding the shrine of St Peter, though on a more massive scale. Both the dimensions and the spiral columns of St Peter's had been referenced in English churches for centuries – the crypts at Hexham and Ripon are scaled-down versions of the crypt that housed the relics of St Peter, and the spiral columns of the shrine were imitated at Ripon – but these earlier buildings pale in comparison to the size of Durham and the massiveness of its piers. Unique to architecture built in the new style are the deep galleries that span the entire width of the side aisles, as well as the clerestory fronted by an interior wall passage. The nave rises to an impressive 73 feet (22 metres), and the twinned towers of the eastern and western facades, along with the central crossing tower, added to the building's impressive scale. The cathedral's unusually wide gallery and central staircases may have been designed to accommodate troops should the complex come under attack.[41] Durham's architecture was copied on a smaller scale in the early twelfth-century Lindisfarne Priory, linking the original home of the Cuthbert community to the cathedral, and at Dunfermline Abbey, built by Malcolm III and Margaret in the late eleventh century. Dunfermline can be read, on the one hand, as a statement of Scottish allegiance to William after his defeat of Edgar Ætheling and, on the other, as a sign of Malcolm and Margaret's long-standing devotion to St Cuthbert and support of the pre-Norman community in Durham.[42]

In many ways Durham exemplifies the complex world of early medieval England. The Cuthbert community had its origins in the Christianity of the Irish church that was embraced in the North before the 663/4 Synod of Whitby decided in favour of Rome. In details of its plan and structure, the new cathedral commemorated Rome and the foundation of the Roman church. It housed the shrine of Cuthbert, arguably the greatest national saint, and the bones of Bede, England's first historian. It had been founded by the monks who fled Lindisfarne after the first wave of Viking invasions, yet it maintained a complex political and economic relationship with York and Scandinavian leaders in the north.[43] It was a monument to both pre-Conquest history and to the new Norman rulers who began the construction of the cathedral-castle complex that survives today. Its fortified appearance is a testament both to Norman control and to the united northern resistance of the English, Scots, and Danes. That appearance is due not only to Norman architectural innovation and ambition but also to the way in which the cathedral and castle seem to rise up out of the rock of the peninsula on which they are built so that the rock of the land and the architectural structure become one. The

[41] Klukas, 'Architectural Implications', 151–65; Thurlby, 'Roles of the Patron', 173–4.

[42] On Dunfermline, see Cameron, 'Romanesque Sculpture'; Fernie, 'Romanesque Churches'; Fawcett, 'Dunfermline Abbey Church'.

[43] See Johnson-South, *Historia de Sancto Cuthberto*.

integration of material into the materiality of works of art is the subject of the next section.

2 Materials and Materiality

The materials that works of art and architecture were made from in early medieval England mattered a great deal and can have much to say about the idea of England as it was coming into formation. Different materials, like different animals, were believed to have differing qualities and agencies, a belief based in classical learning. Texts such as Pliny the Elder's Latin *Natural History* and the (originally) Greek *Physiologus* attributed symbolic and/or moral and medicinal qualities to animals, plants, stones, and other elements of the natural world. The lion, for example, was believed to sleep with its eyes open and hence became a symbol of the ever-watchful Christ. In the early seventh century Isidore of Seville collected and summarised many of these ideas in his *Etymologiae*, a work that was extremely popular across early medieval Europe. He wrote, for example, that the *astrion*, which is 'quite close to crystal, is from India, and in its centre a star shines with the gleam of the full moon. It takes its name because when held facing the stars it catches their gleam and casts it back.'[44] Riddles also conveyed the agency of things. The quill pen moving across the page was a white bird leaving black tracks in a field of snow,[45] and the skin of the parchment page describes the experience of its transformation from a living being into a living book in Exeter Book Riddle 26.[46] Of course, not every work of art foregrounds the symbolism of its materials or the agency of the object, but the number that do indicates that this was an important area of early medieval English art.

Equally important is the question of the sound and voice of artworks.[47] Monuments like the eighth-century Ruthwell Cross or the ninth-century Alfred Jewel speak in the first person, but it is their human makers who cause them to speak by inscribing them with voice. The voice of the Ruthwell inscription unites the speaking cross with the speaking/reading human so that both speak as one.

> +ondgeredæ hinæ god almeittig
> þa he walde on galgu gistiga
> modig fore allæ men
> buga [ic ne dorstæ]

---

[44] Barney et al., ed. and trans., *Etymologies*, 326.

[45] Aldhelm, *Enigma* 59, in Bitterli, *Say What I am Called*, 143.

[46] Muir, *Exeter Anthology*, 306–7. Riddle numbers vary across editions, as there is disagreement as to where some riddles begin and end.

[47] See Kay, 'Siren Enchantments'.

ahof ic riicnæ kyniŋc
heafunæs hlafard
hælda ic ni dorstæ
bismærædu uŋket men ba ætgadre
ic wæs miþ blodi bistemid
bi[goten of þæs gumu sida]

+krist wæs on rodi
hweþræ þer fusæ fearran kwomu
æþþilæ til anum ic þæt al biheald
saræ ic wæs miþ sorgum gidrœfid
hnag [ic þam secgum til handa]
miþ strelum giwundad
alegdun hiæ hinæ limwœrignæ gistoddun
him æt his licæs heafdum
bihealdun hiæ þer [heafunes dryctin]

[+Almighty God stripped himself when he wished to mount the gallows, brave in the sight of all men. I dared not bow. I raised aloft a powerful king. The Lord of heaven. I dared not tilt. Men insulted the pair of us together. I was drenched with blood begotten from that man's side. +Christ was on the cross. But eager ones came hither from afar. Noble ones came together. I beheld all that. I was terribly afflicted with sorrows. I bowed to the hands of men, wounded with arrows. They laid him down, limb-weary; they stood at the shoulders of the corpse. They looked upon the Lord of heaven.]

The sound of the voice in this case becomes the medium through which the eternal and the ephemeral, place and time, rub up against each other. What would it mean to listen for the sound of the material itself, or the sound of the object as it resonates with its embodied human users? The making of sculpture – indeed the making of all works – involved sound, though how that would have been experienced by the artists or their patrons is largely undocumented. One exception is the making of manuscripts in which riddles such as Exeter Book Riddles 26 and 51 encourage readers to imagine the sounds of the living creatures whose skins and feathers became the parchment and quills that were essential parts of manuscript production. Riddle 26 also describes the ripping of flesh from an animal and the scraping of the flayed skin as it was turned into the pages of a book. Michelle M. Sauer's study of sound and parchment has documented the different tones of 'singing' parchment that result from the scraping of different types, ages, and thicknesses of animal skin,[48] but the play of sound and silence in the texts and images that cover those skins merits more attention. We read the tearing, dismembering, and

---

[48] See https://soundstudiesblog.com/2016/10/17/audiotactility-the-medieval-soundscape-of-parchment/.

silencing of the bodies of the Vices in the late-tenth- or early-eleventh-century C.C.C.C. MS 23 copy of Prudentius's *Psychomachia* very differently if we read them through the torn, dirtied, and silenced animal of the parchment compared to if we read them as just words or drawings on a page. The threat of the partially sub-human, dark, and revolting Grendel and his mother in *Beowulf* becomes much more visceral if we read them as silently lurking within the silenced animal skin of the folios than if we think of them as just words on a page or figures evoked solely through those words.[49] Grendel and his mother are figures of the colonised, their land taken from them by the Danes, and the colonised cannot speak. Adam Miyashiro has demonstrated the way in which the runic character *eþel*, the word *eþel* (ancestral homeland), the acts of writing and speaking, and the act of dismembering with a sword come together in the poem to erase the already silenced Grendelkin.

> The runic characters appear during important speech acts (such as battle speeches, commemorations, and boasts), linking the idea of 'ancestral homeland' with the symbol of sovereign violence through the image of the sword, and suggesting that the dismemberment of language in *Beowulf* can be extended to writing as well as speech, as Susan M. Kim argues . . . . Notably, the verb *writan*, apart from being the antecedent of the modern 'to write', also means 'to cut', 'engrave', or 'incise.' The latter is associated with the Latin *scribere* and the Greek *glyphos* – this aspect of cutting into/away from wood, stone, metal reflects the dismemberment of language in *Beowulf* in *writing*, literalized in the bodily dismemberments of Grendel and his mother.[50]

There is a long history of equating the colonised with the bestial and the subhuman, which in England can be traced back to Gildas, who described the Scots and Picts as worms who wriggled out of fissures in the rocks.[51] In the case of *Beowulf*, the materiality of the skin on which the poem is written helps to figure the Grendelkin neatly into that tradition.

Some books were made into talking objects. The verse *Preface* to King Alfred's translation of Gregory the Great's *Regula Pastoralis* speaks in the first-person voice of the book, saying,

Ðis ærendgewrit   Agustinus

ofer sealtne sæ   suðan brohte

iegbuendum,   swa hit ær fore

---

[49] I use the term 'revolting' in the dual sense of the word elaborated by Rambaran-Olm, Leake, and Goodrich, 'Medieval Studies'. Grendel and his mother are at once revolting to the Danes and revolting against them.

[50] Miyashiro, 'Homeland Insecurity', 388. See also Kim, '"As I Once Did with Grendel"'; Fleming, 'Eþel-Weard'.

[51] Winterbottom, *Gildas*, 23.

adihtode   Dryhtnes cempa,

Rome papa.   Ryhtspel monig

Gregorius   gleawmod geondwod

durh sefan snyttro,   searoðonca hord . . .

Siððan min on Englisc   Æl[f]fred cyning

awende worda gehwelc,   ⁊ me his writerum

sende suð ⁊ norð . . .

(lines 1–7, 11–13a)

Augustine brought this letter over the salt sea from the south to the island dwellers, just as the Lord's champion, the pope in Rome, had written it earlier. The wise Gregory had studied many noble writings through his wise mind, his hoard of wisdom. Afterwards, King Alfred translated every word of me into English and sent me south and north to his scribes.][52]

The words also do the job of mapping the transmission of the text from Gregory's Rome to Alfred's England via Augustine. In the verse *Epilogue* that ends the translation, the book again speaks but as a body of life-giving water containing divine wisdom:

Ðis is nu se wæterscipe   ðe us weroda God

to frofre gehet   foldbuendum.

He cwæð ðæt he wolde   ðæt on weorulde forð

of ðæm innoðum   a libbendu

wætru fliowen,   ðe wel on hiene

geliefden under lyfte.   Is hit lytel tweo

ðæt ðæs wætersciepes   welsprynge is

on heofonrice;   þæt is Halig Gast.

(lines 1–8)

[This is now the body of water which the God of hosts promised for the comfort of us earth-dwellers. He said that he wished ever-living waters to flow continually in the world from the hearts of those under the sky who fully believed in him. There is little doubt that the source of the body of water is in the kingdom of heaven, that is, the holy ghost.][53]

---

[52] Schreiber, *King Alfred's Old English Translation*, 197–8; translation my own. See also Discenza, 'Alfred's Verse Preface'.

[53] Schreiber, *King Alfred's Old English Translation*, 451; trans. Irvine and Godden in Irvine, 'The Alfredian Prefaces', 159 n52.

Sacred books contained the living words of scripture passed directly from God through the evangelists to the scribes who produced the manuscripts. This process is documented in the colophon to the early-eighth-century Lindisfarne Gospels (London, BL, Cotton MS Nero D.iv).[54] The colophon was added in the tenth century, along with a gloss on the main text, by the scribe Aldred while the manuscript and the Cuthbert community were at Chester-le-Street, but it contains a section of much earlier verse perhaps copied from the now-missing cover of the manuscript.[55] It opens with a Latin inscription written to the right of the explicit to John's gospel: '+ Lit[er]a me pandat sermonis fida ministra. Omnes alme meos fratres voce salvta [+ May the letter, faithful servant of the word, speak for me. Greet all my brothers with a kindly voice]'.[56] This is followed by the 'Five sentences' in alternating lines of Old English and Latin which state that Matthew wrote from the word of Christ, Mark from the word of Peter, Luke from the word of Paul, and John from the word of God and the Holy Spirit. Then follows Aldred's account of this gospel book, which includes what is believed to be the earlier inscription.

+ eadfrið bisco[p/b] lindisfearnensis æcclesiæ
he ðis boc avrát æt frvma gode ⁊ s[an]c[t]e
cvðberhte ⁊ allvm ðæm halgvm. ða 'gimænelice' ðe
in eolonde sint. ⁊ eðilvald lindisfearneolondinga 'bisc[op]'
hit vta giðryde ⁊ gibélde sva hé vel cuðę.
⁊ billfrið se oncrę he gismioðade ða
gihríno ða ðe ðe vtan ón sint ⁊ hit gi <->
hrínade mið golde ⁊ mið gimmvm ęc
mið svlfre' of[er]gylded faconleas feh:
⁊ [ic] Aldred p[res]'s'b[yte]r indignus ⁊ misserim[us]
mið godes fvltv[m]mę ⁊ s[an]c[t]i cvðberhtes
hit of[er]glóesade ón englisc ⁊ hine gihamadi
mið ðæm ðríim dælv[m]. Mathevs dǽl
gode ⁊ s[an]c[t]e cvðberhti. Marc[vs] dǽl.
ðæm bisc[ope]. ⁊ lvcas dæl ðæm hiorode
⁊ æht 'v' ora s[eo \'v']lfres mið tó inláde.:-
⁊ sci ioh[annes] dæl f[ore] hine seolfne 'i[d est] f[or]e his savle' ⁊ feover óra
s[eo]'v'lfres mið gode ⁊ s[an]c[t]i cvðberti. Þ[æt]te he
hæbbe ondfong ðerh godes miltsæ on heofnv[m].
séel ⁊ sibb on eorðo forðgeong ⁊ giðyngo
visdóm ⁊ snyttro ðerh s[an]c[t]i cvðberhtes earnvnga: ⁊
+eadfrið. oeðilvald. billfrið. Aldred.
hoc evange[lium] d[e]o ⁊ cuðberhto constrvxer[vn]t '[ve]l ornavervnt.

---

54 See www.bl.uk/manuscripts/FullDisplay.aspx?index=14&ref=Cotton_MS_Nero_D_IV.
55 Roberts, 'Aldred Signs Off'.
56 The transcription is based on that in Roberts, 'Aldred Signs Off'.

['+ Eadfrith, bishop of the Lindisfarne church, first wrote this book for God and St Cuthbert, and all the saints whose relics are in the island. And Eðilwald, bishop of the Lindisfarne islanders, pressed it and covered it on the outside as well he knew how to do. And Billfrið the anchorite made the metal ornaments that are on the outside and decorated it with gold and with gems and also with gilded over silver – pure treasure. And [I] Aldred, unworthy and most miserable priest, glossed it in English with the help of God and St Cuthbert and made a home for himself with these three sections: the section of Matthew was for God and St Cuthbert, the section of Mark for the bishop, the section of Luke for the members of the community together with eight ores of silver for his induction, and the section of John for himself, i.e. for his soul, together with four ores of silver for God and St Cuthbert so that, through the mercy of God, he may gain acceptance into heaven, happiness and peace on earth, success and progress, wisdom and knowledge through the reward of St Cuthbert.

+Eadfrið, Oeðilwald, Billfrið and Aldred made this gospel book for God and St Cuthbert.]

The sacredness of the words of the gospels are captured not only in the scribal genealogy of the colophon but also in the 'pure metal' and gems of its original cover. The exterior cover was also reflected in the rich mineral pigments and gilded details of the illuminated pages within.

The Lindisfarne Gospels is renowned for its evangelist portraits, the earliest surviving writing evangelists in Western manuscript illumination, but it is its great carpet and incipit pages that visually express its animality (Figure 6). The cross-carpet pages, the designs of which may have been influenced by Coptic art, are filled with backgrounds of entangled and spiralling birds and beasts against which geometric shapes and cross patterns stand out. The tight, almost symmetrical, order of the carpet pages reflects the order of God's creation, but on the incipit pages the letters and designs in some instances appear ready to crawl off the page. The ascenders of the first three letters of the *Liber* of Matthew's gospel on folio 27r end in stylised serpent heads formed from patterns derived from contemporary metalwork. Each head has two roundels for eyes, and the tops of the letters 'L' and 'b' sprout ears or horns on either side of the eyes, while their mouths end in curling tusks. The sinuous shapes of these letters make them appear as if they are uncoiling and about to slither away; however, all three letters are joined together by birds or geometric ornament at the points that their bodies cross, effectively anchoring them to the page and preventing their escape. A little animal rises from the left-hand side of the lower border, arching its head back in awe of the spectacle taking place before it.

Most discussions of the materiality of manuscripts focus on the living skin of the book and the traces of its readers but, as the Lindisfarne Gospels makes clear, other materials – gold, silver, gems – were also a part of that materiality. In the dedication

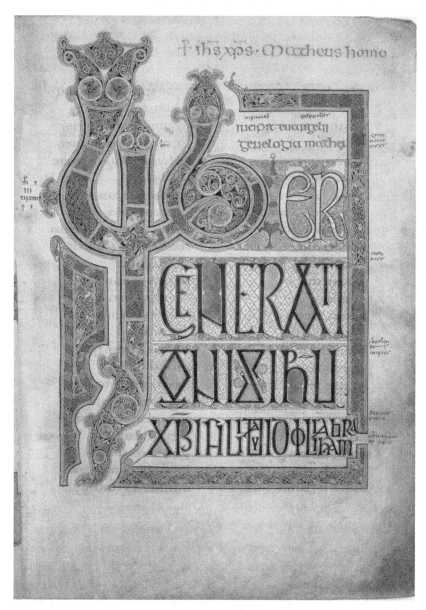

Figure 6 Lindisfarne Gospels, Incipit to Matthew, London, British Library,
Cotton MS Nero D.iv, fol. 27r. Wikimedia Commons/public domain.

to the Benedictional of St Æthelwold (London, BL, Additional MS 49598) produced
in Winchester 971–84, the scribe Godeman records that Æthelwold specified that he
wanted his book to include 'many arches well adorned and filled with various figures
decorated with numerous beautiful colors and with gold'.[57] A benedictional contains

---

[57] Deshman, *Benedictional of Æthelwold*, 148.

blessings used by a bishop during the mass, and this one is a highly personal and lavish manuscript with twenty-eight full-page figures of saints and biblical scenes for feast days all set within gilded frames, most filled with acanthus ornament, as well as ornate gilded initials and incipits to the texts.[58] The saints depicted were important to Æthelwold: Æthelthryth of Ely (fol. 90v), Swithun of Winchester (fol. 97v), and St Benedict (fol. 99v), whose Rule was used in Æthelwold's reformation of English monasteries. The final blessing is for the dedication of a church, and the accompanying miniature shows a bishop, believed to be Æthelwold himself, conducting a service before a congregation of laypeople and monks (fol. 118v). The bishop stands behind a purple-draped altar and reads from a golden book as he blesses the group before him. Gold and coloured inks are used to set the sacred space of the altar and the chancel arch apart from the space of the congregation. The altar area is sacred space, and the bishop reads blessings that have their ultimate authority in God, so colour is used to distinguish this from the everyday world of the congregation represented in monochrome outline drawing against a plain vellum background. Like the animals from which the pages of the book come, these people are of lesser status and distinct from the animals only through their belief in the teachings of the Christian religion. The golden book held in the bishop's left hand extends into their space as a demonstration of this truth.

A similar but more complex use of style and materials to indicate the interpenetration of different spaces is seen in the miniature of St Benedict with the monks of Canterbury in the 1012–23 Eadui Psalter (London, BL, Arundel MS 155; Figure 7).[59] Here the enthroned saint and arched space in which he sits are fully painted with ink washes of reds, blues, and greens with gold leaf details. Benedict is unmoving and looks directly out at the reader. At right, outline drawing has been used to depict the monks of Canterbury, who are very much of this world. Their active profile poses and the dynamic lines of their drapery contrast with Benedict's rigid frontality. The leading monk offers the saint a copy of the Benedictine Rule held open to the first words of its text. It is unclear whether Benedict has just presented the Rule to the monks or whether they are presenting a copy to him, and it may be that the book is intended to represent the idea that the group is united in the text of the Rule. Other objects intended to honour the saint (a book and a pyx) are picked out in gold leaf. At the bottom of the miniature, a prostrate monk kisses Benedict's slippers and presents him with a book inscribed 'lib ps' (*liber psalmorum*), representing this manuscript. This monk is thought by many to be the Canterbury scribe Eadui Basan, who wrote the text of this manuscript and may also have been its

[58] See www.bl.uk/manuscripts/FullDisplay.aspx?ref=Add_MS_49598.
[59] See www.bl.uk/manuscripts/FullDisplay.aspx?index=83&ref=Arundel_MS_155.

Figure 7 Portrait of the monks of Canterbury with St Benedict, London, British
Library, Arundel MS 155, fol. 133r. Wikimedia Commons/public domain.

artist.[60] His belt is inscribed in Latin with the words 'zone of humility'. The fact
that Eadui is depicted, or has depicted himself, in full colour and in the same
space as Benedict may indicate that he was anything but humble, but it is more
likely intended to invoke a scribal genealogy similar to that documented in the
colophon of the Lindisfarne Gospels. Eadui has written the words of the psalter
in thanks for the words of the Rule written by the saint and, through this process,
enters briefly into the spiritual realm of the saint himself. At top, the hand of
God descends with a scroll that, like the books held by Eadui and the unidentified

---

[60] Karkov, *Art of Anglo-Saxon England*, 205–7.

Canterbury monk, bridges heavenly and earthly space. The side above Benedict reads 'Qui vos audit, me audit' (Luke 10.16: 'He who hears you hears me'), and the side towards the monks 'Obedientes estote preposti u[est]ro' ('be obedient to your superior'), words that echo those of the Rule and are embodied in the actions of Eadui and his brothers. The exchange of texts and learning depicted were clearly important to the community as arches above the tables giving the date of Easter and other liturgical information contain drawings of Pachomius receiving a scroll from an angel (fol. 9v) and a group of tonsured book-holding monks engaged in conversation, presumably about their texts (fol. 10r).

Bone and ivory are also taken from living creatures and retain something of the nature of the creatures from which they came. Elephants, for example, were believed to be chaste and the enemies of serpents,[61] and for both reasons they became associated with purity and the Virgin Mary. Along with its rarity and preciousness, this made elephant ivory an appropriate material for reliquaries and the covers of sacred books. Elephant ivory wasn't available in early medieval England after the Arab expansions of the seventh century curtailed trade, so walrus ivory and, less frequently, whalebone were used instead. Both walruses and whales were dangerous and violent creatures, very different from the pure and protective elephant. The whale was particularly fearsome. The fisherman in Ælfric's tenth-century *Colloquy* states that he does not hunt whales because a whale could kill him and his companions with a single blow.[62] The whale's jaws were also equated with the gates of hell, as recorded in the poem *The Whale*.[63] Jonah likened the belly of the whale that swallowed him to hell, but the whale was also the vehicle of his salvation, and both the story of Jonah and images of whales appear on sacred objects during the Early Christian period. There is a whale on the fifth-century chalice from Northumbria discussed in Section 1, and Jonah is depicted being swallowed by and emerging from the mouth of the whale on the fourth-century Brescia Casket made in northern Italy and now in the Museo di Santa Giulia at San Salvatore, Brescia, Italy. The Brescia Casket is made of elephant ivory, however, and not whalebone, and it is decorated with relief carvings of scenes from the Old and New Testaments. It is indisputably a Christian object. The Brescia Casket is often cited as a possible model for the Franks Casket (Figure 8) made in eighth-century Northumbria, but the Franks Casket is made from whalebone, probably from the jawbones of a whale, as those would have been the only bones of the right size and shape for its panels. Only one Christian scene appears on its five carved panels, the Adoration of the Magi, on one half of the front panel. It is thus a much more problematic sort of object. The iconographic programme consists of Weland the Smith at his forge and the

---

[61] Barney et al., *Etymologies*, 252.   [62] Ælfric, *Colloquy*, 29–30.

[63] Muir, *The Exeter Anthology*, vol. 1, 272–3.

Figure 8 Franks Casket, front panel, British Museum. © Getty Images.

Adoration of the Magi (front), an archer defending an enclosure from an attacking army (lid), the sack of the temple in Jerusalem and flight of the Jews (back), Romulus and Remus suckled by the she-wolf (left side), and a cryptic scene involving humans, animals, and hybrid creatures (right side).[64] Aside from the lid, much of which is missing, each panel is surrounded by an inscription. Most are in the Old English language and runic alphabet, although the back panel includes a phrase in Latin and the Roman alphabet, and the final word of the inscription on the back is in Latin and runes. The inscription on the front reads,

> fisc flodu ahof   on fergenberig
>
> warþ ga:sric grorn   þær he ongreut giswom.
>
> hronæs ban.

[The fish beat up the seas [or rose by means of the sea] onto the high hill [or cliff, or burial mound]. The king of terror [or one strong in life or power] became sad when he swam aground onto the shingle. Whale's bone[s].]

The words inscribed in the lower border of this panel are carved retrograde.[65]

Scholarship on the Franks Casket is extensive, and there is no agreement on what its original function or meaning(s) were. Recent studies have understood it as having multiple possible interpretations rather than a single overall theme or message,[66] although some still believe that it may have been a reliquary carrying a message of religious synchronism or harmony. It was clearly important to its makers, however, that it was made of whalebone and that viewers knew that, as the inscription describing the stranding of the whale and the statement that this is whalebone are carved on the front panel, the panel on which we would expect to find the most important image and inscription. Looking more closely at this panel, its division into two may be its most important feature, reflecting the two opposing natures of the whale, the jaws of hell and a vehicle of salvation. The two figural scenes pull away from each other, the movement in the Weland panel being from right to left and that in the Adoration of the Magi from left to right. The whale is also divided in two, at one moment a powerful living creature beating up the sea and in the next a dead mass of bones on the shore. The double meaning of *ferginberig* locates the dead whale as simultaneously visible on a high cliff and on (or in) a burial mound. Even the term used for the whale is divided in two. Just beneath the bird leading the Magi are two

---

[64] For high resolution images of all panels, see www.britishmuseum.org/collection/object/H_1867-0120-1. The right-side panel here is a replica. The original is in the Bargello Museum in Florence.

[65] For the other inscriptions, see Karkov, *Imagining Anglo-Saxon England*, 85–8.

[66] Karkov, *Imagining Anglo-Saxon England*, 77–124; Paz, *Nonhuman Voices*, 98–138; Webster, *Franks Casket*.

dots dividing the word *gasric* in two: 'ga:sric'. More generally, the casket displays three scenes from the Mediterranean world of Rome and three from northern Europe. It may be that some sort of harmony or resolution is possible, but these are all scenes, or excerpts from stories, centred on terror, sadness, and violence. Ultimately, like the whale, the Casket offers no resolution and no definitive narrative. The late eighth-century whalebone Gandersheim Casket in the Herzog Anton Ulrich Museum, Braunschweig, Germany, doesn't exploit its material in anything like the same way, but it too has no indisputably Christian meaning, although its panels filled with creatures are neatly divided into patterns of three, six, and twelve and are thought to symbolise God's creation.

These two boxes aside, whalebone was rarely used for luxury objects,[67] but walrus ivory was. It was the material used by the English for a range of sacred objects from reliquaries such as the mid-eleventh-century openwork reliquary in the V&A to the bodies of Christ, Mary, and John in scenes of the Crucifixion.[68] Walrus ivory was imported from Scandinavia, as recounted by the Norse trader Ohthere in the Alfredian version of Orosius's *Universal History Against the Pagans*. Ohthere tells Alfred that he went north to the territory of the Finnas and Beormas (Saami and Biarmians) both to explore and because the walruses in the area have very fine tusks, some of which he presented to the king.[69]

Walrus ivory was used for a mid-eleventh-century box believed to be a pen case now in the British Museum,[70] and something of the nature of the walrus (*horshwæl*) may be manifest in its design and decoration. Walruses were valuable but also dangerous creatures and are amongst the sea monsters on medieval maps. The ends of the box are carved with open beast-mouths with pronounced teeth or tongue-like appendages. Little creatures about to be eaten squirm in the beasts' mouths. Along the sides of the box dragons, men, birds, and quadrupeds hunt each other and search for food. The spine of the lid is a tree-of-life motif filled with more gobbling creatures that may represent the abundance of the world. The motifs can be related to the function of the box as a container with the gobbling creatures all in the process of consuming and containing. If it was a pen case, the box would have held quill pens, and the two archers shooting at birds on one of its sides might have been reflective of its function. Its function and imagery can also be read in the context of Exeter Book

[67] Riddler, 'Archaeology of the Anglo-Saxon Whale'.

[68] For the V&A reliquary (A.6-1966) see http://collections.vam.ac.uk/item/O96379/reliquary-cross-unknown/. See also the c.1000 ivory corpus of Christ set on an Ottonian reliquary cross in the V&A (7943-1862), https://collections.vam.ac.uk/item/O111551/reliquary-cross-crucifix-unknown/.

[69] Godden, *Old English History of the World*, 36–9. Ohthere also describes whale hunting in the area.

[70] See www.britishmuseum.org/collection/object/H_1870-0811-1.

Riddle 51 in which a pen held in a scribe's fingers leaves tracks across the page, a metaphor for the production and understanding of knowledge, the *ruminatio*, of early medieval texts.

The late-ninth-century Alfred Jewel is also associated with manuscript culture.[71] The Jewel is generally identified as an *æstel*, probably a book pointer of the type that Alfred distributed to his bishops with copies of his translation of the *Regula Pastoralis*, although that identification is not certain and other uses for the Jewel have been suggested. Nevertheless, the circumstantial evidence for the Jewel's association with Alfred's court – its date, quality, find spot near Athelney, and inscription – is considerable. The Jewel consists of an enamelled figure set on a base-plate of gold and covered with a reused Roman rock crystal, the whole secured by an inscribed open-work gold band terminating in a golden animal head socket. The inscription reads 'Ælfred mec heht gewyrcan' ('Alfred ordered me to be made'). The reused Roman crystal had imperial as well as Christological connections, both it and gold were materials associated with light and learning as well as with kings, and for these reasons such an object would have appealed to Alfred and his vision of expanding his kingdom. The enamel figure with its wide, staring eyes may be a personification of Sight or Wisdom, an image of Christian learning, and/or a portrait of the king. It could allude to all these things at once. In addition to its associations with Rome, the crystal covering the figure was symbolic of Christ both because of the Old English word for the stone, *cristesmæl/cristelmæl*, and because of the writings of figures like Isidore and Gregory the Great.[72] Gold was precious but also symbolic of purity and the divine light of heaven. Despite the fact that neither the Jewel's association with the king nor its function as a book pointer is certain, the material and imagery of the Jewel are undeniably centred on light, clarity, sight, and authority and would thus be appropriate to an object that brought together mind, eye, and hand in the pursuit of wisdom. The inscription's first-person voice draws attention to the meaning and agency of the Jewel, and its wording is similar to the lines from the verse Preface to the *Regula Pastoralis* cited earlier, even if it omits the title 'king'. The Jewel is one of a number of objects identified as book pointers, all of which are designed with a central 'eye', although they are not as ornate or complex in their iconography as the Alfred Jewel. The Bowleaze Cove Jewel has a circular gold head with a central blue bead, and the Warminster Jewel's head consists of a central blue bead set in a circular rock crystal, while the top of the Yorkshire *æstel* is an animal head with staring eyes.

---

[71] Ashmolean Museum, University of Oxford AN1836 p.135.37.
[72] Gregory the Great, *Homiliae in Hiezechihelem*, 95; Kempshall, 'No Bishop, No King', 127.

While the materiality of metalwork was exploited for expressions of personal identity, stone spoke about the identity of time and place, as the material
comes from the land and could be used and reused to establish specific
relationships to the past. Wilfrid's reuse of Roman stone in the building of
Hexham was as much a part of his statement of Northumbrian *romanitas* as
was his modelling of the crypt at Ripon on that of Old St Peter's.[73] Scholarship
on the materiality of stone and its ability to express political or religious
identity and affiliation is enormous, particularly for sculpture and structures
of the seventh and eighth centuries, like Hexham, or the eighth-century
crosses at Ruthwell and Bewcastle. The latter have been discussed in terms
of their proclamation of allegiance to the Roman world and the origins of the
Roman church; the stone of Bewcastle is linked to that of Bewcastle's Roman
fort, still partially standing when the cross was erected; and Ruthwell uses
stone to unite eighth-century Northumbria and first-century Jerusalem across
the centuries.[74] Less well studied is the agency of stone in Anglo-
Scandinavian sculpture, with the notable exception of Howard Williams's
work on hogbacks and the 'mnemonics of their materiality'. The hogback's
form, he demonstrates, holds together a set of allusions to other types of
structures such as halls and shrines, while their combination of form and
material creates a unique lithic solidity. They are solid, closed, fixed in
place, a secure home for the dead; yet an architecture that is simultaneously
open in its multiple allusions to other forms of monument and other times and
places.[75]

A related combination of lithic solidity that opens itself out in a rather
different way can be seen in the tenth-century Dearham Cross, Cumbria
(Figure 9). The cross appears to be a solid block of stone covered with variations
on ring-chain ornament of a distinctively Anglo-Scandinavian type.[76] A similar
pattern covers the lowest section of the shaft of the Gosforth Cross, from the first
half of the tenth century, and the pattern may represent the strapwork of leather
armour, with the cross becoming both a protected object and a type of armed
warrior ready for battle.[77] The most remarked-upon aspect of the Dearham
Cross is the bulb-like form near the base of the shaft that is carved as if it is
emerging out from the stone of the cross to bury itself in the ground. This root
anchors the cross in place and reinforces the idea that the cross is a living object.

---

[73] Bidwell, 'Survey of the Anglo-Saxon Crypt'; Karkov, 'Alternative Histories'.

[74] Ó Carragáin, *Ritual and the Rood*; Orton and Wood, with Lees, *Fragments of History*; Karkov,
'Alternative Histories'; Karkov, *Art of Anglo-Saxon England*, 136–45.

[75] Williams, 'Hogbacks and the Materiality of Solid Spaces'.

[76] See https://chacklepie.com/ascorpus/catvol2.php?pageNum_urls=80.

[77] Karkov, *Art of Anglo-Saxon England*, 258.

Figure 9 Dearham Cross, Cumbria. © Corpus of Anglo-Saxon Stone
Sculpture, photographer Tom Middlemass.

Far from being an inanimate piece of stone, blood or sap courses through its
interior.[78] The Dearham Cross is not covered with blood like the Ruthwell
Cross, as described in the Ruthwell runic poem, nor with blood and gold like the
visionary cross in the poem *The Dream of the Rood*, preserved in the c.1000
Vercelli Book, although like those crosses it becomes two things at once, in this

---

[78] The idea of the cross as a tree with its roots reaching into the ground may refer to either or both
Christ as the cosmic tree or the Scandinavian Yggdrasill; see https://chacklepie.com/ascorpus/
catvol2.php?pageNum_urls=80.

case stone and wood. But, unlike those crosses, it does not speak in the first person: its materiality is conveyed solely through its materials and its setting in the earth.

Stone and the multiple possible statements it could make about place and identity had thus been a feature of early medieval English sculpture, architecture, and landscape for centuries. It is no surprise, then, that the Cuthbert community finally settled in Durham after travelling around England for over 100 years. The prominence of the Durham peninsula provided a ready-made statement about the power of the saint who had become so closely identified with the North, with the English church, and with England. Like the island of Lindisfarne from which they had fled at the end of the ninth century, it was a rock on which a church – a new church that expressed continuity with the origins of the community – could be built. The setting, like the architecture of the later Norman cathedral and castle discussed previously, proclaimed both a link to the past and a new power and order built upon the previous one. In the ninth through eleventh centuries, it was a statement that could appeal differently to the old English and Anglo-Scandinavian inhabitants, while with the building of the new cathedral in the 1080s, the site expressed both continuity with the past and the power of the new Norman settlers and overlords in equal measure. It spoke of a very complex layering of time, land, identity, and a formation of England that was both profoundly local and national, yet also international as it became part of the new Norman Empire. The final section of this Element will explore England's place in that larger empire, but first I will turn to the question of how art was used to express more personal ideas of identity and allegiance, as well as what we know of the men and women who produced these artworks.

3 Identity and Performance

The materials and types of jewellery and other adornment that were used to convey ethnic and regional identities, and/or political or cultural affiliations, varied over time.[79] Some items, like beads, have been found in the graves of men, women, and children – although they were worn mostly by women and girls from the fifth century on. Beads are important in archaeology but are rarely considered worth discussing by art historians, even though some beads were amongst the most exotic yet widely circulating types of ornament in the early medieval world.[80] The most common materials for beads in early medieval England were glass, amber, stones such as amethyst or jet, rock crystal, gold,

---

[79] On dress and adornment, see Owen-Crocker, *Dress in Anglo-Saxon England*.

[80] Green, 'Indo-Pacific Beads' and sources cited therein.

and silver. The popularity and availability of these materials varied over time. Amber, for example, was common in the fifth and sixth centuries but began to disappear in the seventh. Some beads, or the materials to make them, were imported, with others made from local materials; in some instances, as with amber, there is evidence of both imports and exploitation of local sources. Roman materials were reused, especially for the rarer or more exotic beads such as some of those of rock crystal or glass, and some beads were clearly heirlooms and/or valued for their age or associations. The woman in Grave 43 at Street House, Loftus, North Yorkshire, for example, wore a pendant with a reworked Iron Age bead.[81] Some materials were also believed to have had medicinal or protective powers. Amber was a cure for a wide range of ailments,[82] while, according to Pliny, amethyst prevented drunkenness and protected against evil spells.[83] In the fifth–sixth centuries, women commonly wore beads strung between brooches, but they could also be worn as necklaces. During the seventh–ninth centuries, they were worn most often as necklaces with or without pendants, a fashion ultimately copied from Roman and Byzantine fashions. Other items of women's jewellery included pins, rings, arm-rings, clasps, and buckles, while men wore buckles and clasps, rings, and pins, as well as beads and other decorative items attached to sword belts.

Amethyst beads are amongst the most interesting and are indicative of the extent of the trade routes connecting England to Europe and beyond. The most likely sources of amethysts during the fifth and sixth centuries were India and Sri Lanka, also the source of the garnets that feature so prominently in more lavish items, although other sources might have included Egypt, the Near East,[84] Asia Minor, and Greece.[85] Amethyst deposits are also found across Europe and in Ireland, and it is possible that the lighter colour of the amethyst beads that began to appear in the late seventh century is evidence of the exploitation of local sources as the spread of Islam closed trade routes from India and Africa. The origins and distribution patterns of amethyst beads open the question of whether the ultimate source of their popularity was in Romano-Byzantine fashions or whether they are evidence of a more international fashion trend with origins in the eastern Mediterranean.[86]

Amongst the items found in women's burials throughout the fifth through seventh centuries are ivory rings believed to be bag-rings, supports from which a cloth bag would have been suspended, although some might have been worn

---

[81] Manion, 'Symbolism, Performance and Colour', 152.
[82] Owen-Crocker, *Dress in Anglo-Saxon England*, 150.   [83] Drauschke, 'Byzantine Jewellery?'
[84] A cowrie shell of Near Eastern origin was found in grave 238 at Sarre, Kent: Huggett, 'Imported Grave Goods', 72.
[85] Drauschke, 'Byzantine Jewellery?', 51–2.   [86] Drauschke, 'Byzantine Jewellery?', 58.

as bracelets or have been used for the suspension of things other than bags.[87] Originally thought to have been made from the tusks of either or both walruses and elephants, along with fossil mammoth ivory, scientific analysis of fragments from cremation burials and the size (some greater than 15 cm in diameter) and colour of surviving examples from inhumations show them to be predominantly, if not exclusively, made from elephant ivory. Catherine Hills notes that while we cannot be certain whether the ivory was from Indian or African elephants the most likely source would have been the Christian kingdom of Aksum in Ethiopia; however, the established trade in gemstones from southern India suggests that an Indian source cannot be ruled out altogether. The ivory would, like amethysts and garnets, have travelled via the trade routes that ran from the Indian Ocean through the Red Sea and across the Mediterranean to Europe until the route was closed by Arab expansion.[88] The rings were probably imported ready-carved rather than as unworked tusks, and one ring from a burial at West Heslerton (Yorkshire) was found with fragments of an 'unusual textile' that suggests that it was imported as a finished item.[89] The rings do not come from the wealthiest graves but from the next stratum down and so have received little attention compared to the more flashy and famous items. This also makes them something of a puzzle, as elephant ivory was an exotic material and by the tenth century generally reserved for aristocratic and liturgical items. As Arthur MacGregor notes, the rings do tend to delaminate over time, and many show signs of sometimes repeated repairs,[90] suggesting that they were highly valued by their owners.

There was a certain amount of individual taste in the commissioning and wearing of personal items – especially amongst the elite. We know that people such as Edith of Wilton had a fondness for rich materials and others such as Edith Godwinson for covering her husband in magnificently jewelled apparel because their activities were documented. Both were renowned needlewomen and therefore likely to have worked with personally selected materials and to personal designs. Generally, metalwork and clothing varied regionally, and this has led to the conclusion that they can be used, albeit with caution, to identify ethnic or political identities and affiliations. Regional variation also reveals information about artists' workshops. The gold and garnet jewellery from the early-seventh-century Sutton Hoo Mound 1 burial and some of the sixth- and seventh-century metalwork from the Staffordshire Hoard, for example, are thought to be from the same East Anglian workshop because of the similarities in their materials, style, technique, and quality. A c.600–50 pendant from

[87] Owen-Crocker, *Dress in Anglo-Saxon England*, 69.   [88] Hills, 'Isidore to Isotopes'.
[89] Owen-Crocker, *Dress in Anglo-Saxon England*, 69.
[90] MacGregor, *Bone, Antler, Ivory*. The bag-rings are discussed on 40, 110–12.

a woman's burial at Winfarthing, Norfolk, has also been compared with items from Sutton Hoo and the Staffordshire Hoard because of its quality and intricate design. It was part of a rich assemblage of grave-goods, and, taken as a whole, the burial raises some interesting questions about what sort of identities these three very different assemblages of personal items project.

Sutton Hoo and the Staffordshire Hoard are both much studied, and both have their own websites.[91] They have caught the public imagination in a way that few other finds from early medieval England have, in part because of their scale but also because of the appeal of all that bling. The discovery of each is also connected to significant points in English history. Sutton Hoo, discovered in 1939 on the eve of World War II, received widespread coverage in the press. Francesca Allfrey elucidates how the war, with first its threat of invasion and then the presence of German war planes in English airspace, marked the first time the shores of the island had been invaded since the Middle Ages, and the idea of an English nation, a strong army, and even the beginnings of Empire were projected back onto the burial, especially the helmet.[92] The Staffordshire Hoard was discovered in 2009. A few pieces went on display soon afterwards, and a national tour of highlights from the Hoard followed in 2016. It also received wide press coverage once the find was made public. It too was seen by many as a hoard of treasure won during a battle between kingdoms,[93] although other interpretations have been proposed. This was exactly the period in which pressure for a referendum on UK membership in the European Union was growing, culminating in the Brexit vote of June 2016. The Hoard seemed to speak both to the "origins" of England and to the strength of a kingdom, and it was considered a national treasure. National treasures tend to have particular appeal at times of national crises or crises in national identity, and – with their spectacular war-gear – both Sutton Hoo and the Staffordshire Hoard spoke of strength, defence of the realm, and Englishness, at least in the imagination of many. Ironically, neither the garnets imported from southern Asia nor the Roman, Byzantine, or even Brittonic origins of some of the imagery and technology used in the design and manufacture of many of the objects included in the burial or the hoard received as much attention as what the finds had to say about insular history – although the imported material in Mound 1 eventually came to be seen as evidence of the power and position of early medieval East Anglia. Against this backdrop one might wonder at the timing of the movie of *The Dig*, based on a fictional retelling of the original excavation of Mound 1.[94]

---

[91] See www.nationaltrust.org.uk/sutton-hoo; www.staffordshirehoard.org.uk.

[92] Allfrey, 'Sutton Hoo in Public', chap. 2.

[93] See, for example, Addley, 'One of the Greatest Finds'.

[94] D'Arcens, 'The Dig's Romanticisation'.

The film was released on Netflix in January 2021, just after Brexit had taken effect, and the United Kingdom was suffering some food shortages and delays in import and exports. With its atmospheric rural landscapes, melancholic contemplation of discovery, sacrifice, and loss, buzzing warplanes, and refrain that the discovery was 'Anglo-Saxon' and not 'Viking', the movie evokes a World War II–era spirit. To be clear, I'm not saying that the movie was deliberately released to coincide with Brexit, any more than one could say that Sutton Hoo was deliberately dug up in order to coincide with the start of World War II; rather, I am saying that it is a product of and appeals to the same nostalgic English nationalism that is so much a part of Brexit. At the same time that the movie was in production, the Sutton Hoo Ship's Company was created to finance and build a replica of the burial ship. The company's website evocatively connects the seventh century with the twenty-first and suggests that the ship itself is coming back from the grave to patrol England's waters:

> In the corner of England now called Suffolk, an Anglo-Saxon king's burial ship and treasure lay hidden underground. Dormant for over thirteen centuries in the mysterious Sutton Hoo royal burial ground, all that remained of the ship was a shadow of its former awe-inspiring glory.
>
> Developing the Sutton Hoo story, the King's ship will be resurrected to its full ninety-foot length in The Longshed, Woodbridge. From there it will slip once more into the King's River to grace the waters and tides again, reconnecting our Anglo-Saxon maritime heritage with a modern-day sense of discovery.[95]

There is knowledge to be gained through reconstructing the ship as a way of understanding its engineering, construction, and seaworthiness, but to claim that the 'Anglo-Saxon' past is something that is alive but dormant and needing to be resurrected – or that 'Anglo-Saxon' heritage is 'our' heritage – perpetuates the racist discourse that has come to surround the period. This is not the heritage of everyone living in the United Kingdom.

In addition to wealth, Mound 1 and the Staffordshire Hoard spoke of strength and leadership in the period in which their assemblages were made – although some, if not most, of that may have been aspirational rather than real. Noël Adams has reinterpreted the Sutton Hoo shoulder clasps as fittings based on Lombardic or Byzantine models and used to secure the chest protector of an elite warrior rather than the trappings of an imperial figure.[96] The image is, therefore, that of a top military commander but not that of an emperor or a great king. Moreover, burials are filled by the living rather than the dead and say as much, if not more, about their ideas of self-identity than they do about the

---

[95] See https://saxonship.org.   [96] Adams, 'Sutton Hoo Shoulder Clasps,' 102.

person buried. Mound 1 held a wide array of objects from across Britain, Scandinavia, the Continent, and Byzantium, including the ship in which this Scandinavian-style burial was contained, so clearly this was the burial of someone who, or someone whose people, at least aspired to a cosmopolitan stature. The chamber that held the body contained items that the dead man would need to continue his elite lifestyle in the afterlife, including vessels for eating and drinking and the famous lyre for entertainment. The most personal items were placed on or near the body, including the great gold belt buckle, the purse with its elaborately decorated lid, the sword with its fittings, the shoulder clasps, and the helmet. The relatively intact condition of most of the metalwork decorating these objects suggests that they were worn to impress at court rather than in actual battle, but that has little impact on the message that they were intended to convey.

I do not wish to link Sutton Hoo directly to the poem *Beowulf*, as they are two very different entities, but the poem does use the term *gryre-geatwe*, literally terror-ornaments, to describe the arms and armour of Beowulf and his men, a term that allows insights into the way that these things were perceived in the culture that produced, albeit centuries apart, both the Sutton Hoo helmet and the poem. The Sutton Hoo helmet and the weapons from the Staffordshire Hoard are material manifestations of exactly what *gryre-geatwe* means. The helmet was a beautiful adornment. Its replica in the British Museum shows it as it would originally have appeared, with shining garnets, polished silver, and gilded surfaces.[97] At the same time, it is a type of object that would have been worn in battle and intended to create awe and terror in an enemy. Even in a court setting it would have exuded power and demanded awe. Asa Mittman and Patricia MacCormack identify the warriors who dressed in this type of gear as 'fabulated' men who, when they donned their war-gear, became one with it, transforming into part-human, part-animal, part-superhuman battle machines.[98] The dragons or bird and dragon that cover the wearer's face and the crown of the head are protective symbols, but they also suggest that the wearer takes on some of the power and ferocity of the creatures that cover him. The wings of the dragon/bird that form the helmet's eyebrow guards end in boars' heads with tiny but prominent teeth. The plates that covered the helmet's cap and cheek-pieces are decorated with scenes of armed gods and mounted soldiers trampling defeated enemies beneath their horses' hooves. Tiny gods sit behind the mounted warriors. The surfaces of the face-plate are decorated with beaded patterns and interlaced serpents. The decoration is apotropaic but would also

---

[97] See www.britishmuseum.org/collection/object/H_SHR-2; original helmet: www .britishmuseum.org/collection/object/H_1939-1010-93.

[98] Mittman and MacCormack, 'Rebuilding'.

have suggested that the helmet-wearer and the helmet's creatures and materials were one in battle.

The less famous Sutton Hoo shield was decorated with mounts that created a similar supernatural animal, human, and metalwork battler.[99] Animal heads with inlaid garnet eyes were spaced around the rim, holding the shield's layers together, while the mounts near its centre include a gilt copper-alloy dragon and bird of prey – both examples of Style II animal ornament. The dragon has an open mouth with large fangs like those of the boars' heads on the helmet, and the panels that make up the centre of its body contain interlaced animals – as if, perhaps, it had swallowed these creatures. The bird (Figure 10) has a prominent curving beak and claws. The crest of its head is a dragon with inset garnet eye and open toothy mouth, while its hip joint is a human face worked in garnets set over stamped gold foils (a typically English technique). With its beak and claws facing one way, the open-mouthed crest the other, and the human face looking out at us, this is a creature that is ready to attack in all directions. The helmet and shield were the property of a wealthy leader who wanted to project an image of teratological authority in this life and whose people wanted their leader to embody the same image in the next. The helmet continues to threaten as it has come to stand for all things 'Anglo-Saxon'[100] and has been taken up as both a nationalist and a white supremacist symbol.[101]

The Staffordshire Hoard consists entirely of fragments that decorated arms, armour, and other objects that were carried by or adorned the people and horses that went into battle.[102] It includes over 3,500 pieces of sixth- and seventh-century metalwork and is the largest hoard of gold and silver from the period found in England to date. The date-range of the metalwork indicates either that some pieces were heirlooms that had been handed down for generations or that the objects were collected over time. If the former, the hoard could represent loot taken from defeated troops after battle; if the latter, it was more likely the contents of a court treasury and could have included items given in tribute along with objects taken in war. The blades from the swords and knives were all missing and many objects had been folded or damaged. These things were likely on their way to being taken apart and melted down to become other things – just as the gold and perhaps gold and glass inlays from which many of them are made were almost certainly produced by taking apart and melting down earlier objects.

---

[99] See www.britishmuseum.org/collection/object/H_1939-1010-94.

[100] Williams, 'Fight for Anglo-Saxon'.

[101] It is, for example, one of the symbols of nationalism available on merchandise sold by the group 'We Are the English'.

[102] Fern, et al. *Staffordshire Hoard.*

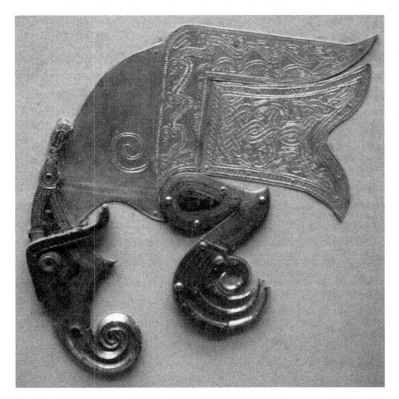

Figure 10 Shield mount from Sutton Hoo, British Museum. © Johnbod/
Wikimedia Commons/CC-BY-SA-3.0/GFDL.

One of the defining features of early medieval English art is that it was almost always in process and rarely, if ever, understood as 'finished'. Metalwork was melted down to be turned into something new, while sculptures, manuscripts, and architecture were reused, re-carved, rebuilt, or added to – as Aldred's gloss was added to the Lindisfarne Gospels, or the Nunburnholme Cross (once a Roman lintel) was carved and re-carved by Anglian, Anglo-Scandinavian, and Anglo-Norman sculptors over the centuries.[103] In whatever way the metalwork of the Staffordshire Hoard was assembled, it makes clear that the taking or collection of *gryre-geatwe* was an expression of victory or power over someone. Sue Brunning has documented the close relationship and entwined identities of warriors and their swords; she suggests that the broken or disfigured state of so many of the hoard weapons may 'reflect an attempt to obliterate a defeated foe – disfiguring, dishonouring and tearing apart sword and owner alike, . . . and in so doing, conferring a final and permanent defeat'.[104] These things that were meant

---

[103] Karkov, 'Postcolonial'.   [104] Brunning, *Sword in Early Medieval Northern Europe*, 87.

to project male strength and create a sense of awe could, then, become signs of loss and defeat rather than victory or power.

The Winfarthing pendant (Figure 11) seems part of a very different world, but this is not necessarily the case. The pendant is of exceptional quality and, while the burial in which it was found has not generated anywhere near the excitement of Sutton Hoo or the Staffordshire Hoard, the UK public voted the pendant their favourite Art Fund–supported museum acquisition of 2018. The central design of a cross formed by five bosses is more commonly found on brooches, and, as on brooches, there are in fact multiple crosses: one on the central boss, one formed by the rectangular garnets that radiate out from the central boss; one formed by the bosses; and one formed by the serpent-filled sections between the bosses. The pendant's surface is covered with cloisonné garnets set onto a sheet of gold. The lidded cloisonné technique, in which cells that would normally hold stones are covered with a lid of gold, was used in the two bands of interlacing serpents that link the bosses

Figure 11 Winfarthing pendant. © Norwich Castle Museum and Art Gallery.

together. Both this technique and the mushroom-shaped garnets of the ring surrounding the serpents appear on some of the metalwork from Sutton Hoo. The Sutton Hoo garnets and similar ones on pieces from the Staffordshire Hoard are more neatly cut and set in their stepped cells, but the overall quality of the pendant is equal to that of the metalwork in those assemblages. The two snakes at right and left in the outer ring of interlaced serpents have tiny garnet eyes, details also found on the Sutton Hoo shoulder clasps and purse lid. On the back of the pendant the ends of the rivets that hold the bosses in place are covered with garnets.

The similarities in technique and imagery raise questions of similarities in meaning. It is possible to understand the brooch, like the Sutton Hoo helmet, as both apotropaic – designed to protect the wearer – and a weapon: the brooch a weapon in the battle between good and evil. It also raises the question of workshops. The pendant has been considered to date from too late in the first half of the seventh century to be the product of the Sutton Hoo workshop, but that implies a scenario in which workshops ended with the death of individual patrons or the decline of individual courts. But artists must have continued to work, and this burial of a young woman is part of a series of East Anglian aristocratic burials that reveal a systematic method of establishing personal status, regional identity, and cultural or historical connections.

The Winfarthing woman was also buried with a crushed Frankish pot, a copper-alloy bowl of foreign manufacture, an iron knife, a set of copper-alloy chatelaine rings that would have hung from her girdle, and a necklace with a gold pendant with a central Maltese cross flanked by two coins of the Frankish king Sigibert III (633–56). Sigibert was also the name of an East Anglian king who took shelter at the Frankish court, but the connection between the two kings remains uncertain. The burial makes a statement about alliances with the Frankish court and is again in this respect connected to Sutton Hoo, where the purse that was part of the burial contained thirty-seven late-sixth-century Frankish coins. It is also connected to the later-seventh- or early-eighth-century burial of an aristocratic woman in grave 93 at Boss Hall, Ipswich, which contained a composite brooch, the front of which was almost completely covered with garnets set in silver with two central crosses, one formed by raised garnets and the other by four triangular sheets of gold decorated with filigree scrollwork set between them. This burial also contained four gold pendants set with garnet and glass, a cabochon pendant set with a single garnet and another set with red glass, a pendant made from a coin of Sigibert III, fragments of biconical spacer beads, a *sceat* dated 690, glass beads, a set of slip-knot rings, and a silver cosmetic set. The artistry of the pendants is not as fine as that of the Winfarthing set, and they may be the

Figure 12 Strickland disc brooch, British Museum. © Jononmac46/Wikimedia Commons/CC-BY-SA-3.0.

product of a workshop in decline.[105] The similarities between the two burials has raised speculation that the women may have been related, or at least part of, the same elite circle,[106] perhaps members or descendants of members of the court of the man buried at Sutton Hoo. Interestingly, while the Sutton Hoo cemetery developed over time, the Boss Hall burial is an intrusion in an earlier sixth–seventh-century cemetery. Perhaps a specific connection with the past was being made, but that too is speculation. The Winfarthing burial is also anomalous as no major settlement or activity is known to have existed in the area, unlike Ipswich which was a political centre.

The use of silver rather than gold for the settings on the Boss Hall brooch is a sign of dwindling gold supplies. As gold became scarcer, the polychrome style of sixth- and seventh-century metalwork was replaced by a more monochrome style, with silver replacing gold and garnets, coloured glass, and enamelwork as the primary aesthetic. The ninth-century Strickland disc brooch (Figure 12) is made of silver inlaid with gold and niello and worked in the Trewhiddle Style, named after a hoard of ninth-century silver coins and other objects discovered at Trewhiddle, Cornwall, in 1774. The use of gold inlay and the intricacy of the design of this brooch distinguishes it as a particularly rich and high-quality item. The lively animals and animal-masks of the ornament may strike viewers first,

---

[105] Webster and Backhouse, *Making of England*, 53.　　[106] Pestell, 'These Burial Treasures'.

but the most important design-element for the wearer was likely its many embedded crosses. One cross is formed by the central lozenge, another by the quatrefoil design surrounding it, another by the raised silver bosses, and perhaps another by the lentoid fields ending in inward-facing animal heads that contain them. While the basic design of multiple crosses combined with animal ornament is retained from the earlier period, the animals have now become individual creatures staring at each other from within discrete niello compartments rather than interlacing together.[107] They may have been apotropaic, as was earlier animal ornament.

On the late-ninth-century Fuller Brooch, the little animals contained within roundels in the brooch's outer ring represent aspects of divine creation in a harmonic whole paralleled and made human by the personifications of the five senses at the brooch's centre.[108] The central figure of Sight can also be interpreted as an allusion to wisdom, and the divine wisdom of which it is a shadow, as the figure is contained within a cruciform field, and there is a tiny niello-filled cross inscribed just beneath the central boss. The wide-staring eyes and foliate branches held by Sight suggest a connection to the enamel figure on the Alfred Jewel, and the two are roughly contemporary. The brooch can be compared with the Strickland Brooch in both quality and certain details of its design; however, where the Strickland Brooch stands apart because of its unusual use of gold inlay, the Fuller Brooch is set apart by its unusual iconography. The Fuller Brooch is silver with niello inlay and an open-work outer ring, creating an aesthetic of light against dark that is characteristic of ninth-century metalwork.

Amongst the most personal of all items were rings, especially seal-rings. A double-sided seal-ring made in northern France but discovered in Postwick, Norfolk, is believed to have been made for the East Anglian Bathilde who married Clovis II, king of the Franks, in 648 (Figure 13) The ring is almost solid gold with a stylised head of the queen beneath a cross and surrounded by the inscription 'BALDEhILDIS' on the obverse. On the reverse is what has been described as an erotic scene of a naked man and woman standing beneath a cross, but the presence of the cross indicates that it should be read within a Christian context. It's possible that this was a wedding ring and the scene on the reverse designed as a particularly intimate image of marriage. Together the ring's two sides could therefore express the two sides of the queen's life, with the public representation of majesty on the display side and an image of her personal life hidden beneath it.

---

[107] See www.britishmuseum.org/collection/object/H_1949-0702-1.
[108] See www.britishmuseum.org/collection/object/H_1952-0404-1.

Figure 13 Bathilde seal matrix, reverse. © Norwich Castle Museum and Art Gallery.

The images on Bathilde's ring are not portraits in the modern sense of the word; that is, they are not physical likenesses of Bathilde but rather images representative of two aspects of her life. It is the inscription alone that suggests the ring was hers. The same is true of the two ninth-century royal rings that survive: those of Æthelwulf, king of Wessex (839–58),[109] and his daughter Æthelswith, queen of Mercia (853–74).[110] Both are made of gold and niello and inscribed with their owners' names: '+ETHELWULF REX' and 'EAÐELSWIÐ REG[I]na'. The king's name and title appear prominently on the front of his ring, but the queen's are inscribed on the underside of the bezel, possibly because the inscription was secondary, or because the design of the ring left no room for the inscription on its top. Both are decorated with Christian imagery in the Trewhiddle style. On the king's ring two peacocks flank a tree of life, while on the queen's ring a quatrefoil design surrounds the lamb of God nimbed and flanked by his monogram. The motifs are undoubtedly meant to convey both the devotion of the two individuals and, more importantly, the sacred nature of their rulership. They may have carried particular royal associations, as they appear elsewhere in art associated with both the courts of the English kingdoms and that of Carolingian France.[111]

---

[109] See www.britishmuseum.org/collection/object/H_1829-1114-1.
[110] See www.britishmuseum.org/collection/object/H_AF-458.
[111] Karkov, *Art of Anglo-Saxon England*, 124–8; Webster, 'Aedificia Nova', 91–4.

Towards the end of the tenth and into the eleventh centuries, there is increasing evidence from both the art-historical and documentary records that the judgment and virtue of kings and queens was questioned.[112] One place in which this is most clearly evident is in the texts of the Nowell Codex of the *Beowulf* manuscript.[113] The manuscript includes a copy of *The Wonders of the East*, a fantastical account of different peoples, creatures, and plants that were believed to exist in a geography including Babylon, India, Egypt, and Ethiopia. The areas covered include those from which the garnets, amethyst, ivory, and, perhaps, some of the beads with which I began this section were imported (India, Ethiopia, and the Red Sea area), so it is fitting to turn to the ways in which these areas were imagined several centuries later at its end. *The Wonders of the East* is derived from the travel narratives and wonder tales of the classical world and was popular in early medieval England, with three different versions of the text surviving: Cotton Vitellius A.xv, fols. 98v–106v (c.1000); London, BL, Cotton MS Tiberius B.xv, 78v–87v (c.1025–50);[114] and Oxford, Bodleian Library, Bodley 614, 34v–52r (mid-twelfth-century).[115] The two pre-Conquest copies of the text are illustrated with very different images, and thus the way in which they envisage the people who inhabit 'the East' is very different. In the Tiberius B.v cycle, humans are dressed as humans, and the non-human, or only partially human, wonders are without clothing or other accoutrements. In Vitellius A.xv, however, some creatures sport human clothing or jewellery. The Homodubii (doubtful- or maybe-men, fol. 102v) who live near the Red Sea, like the Ethiopians (fol. 106v) or the English, wear bracelets or arm-rings. These details suggest that they were perceived as not entirely different from the population of early England but also that the animal and the human are intertwined with each other. Other wonders appear to be naked but, on closer examination, can be seen to be wearing what can only be described as wonder-suits or monster-suits.[116] The body of the famous Blemmye (a headless creature with its face on its chest) is naked on folio 82r of Tiberius B.v but appears to be wearing a transparent tunic with a hem at its knees and a neckline visible above its face on folio 102v of Vitellius A.xv. The Vitellius Blemmye also wears shoes and stockings. Similar details of the edges of sleeves, necklines, or folds of drapery appear on other of the seemingly naked wonders, such as the giant boar-tusked

---

[112] Karkov, 'Conquest and Material Culture'; Treharne, *Living through the Conquest.*

[113] See www.bl.uk/manuscripts/FullDisplay.aspx?ref=Cotton_MS_Vitellius_A_XV.

[114] See www.bl.uk/manuscripts/FullDisplay.aspx?ref=Cotton_MS_Tiberius_B_V/1.

[115] Folios 34v–48r of the Oxford manuscript are a copy of the Tiberius B.v miniatures; the rest of the text and miniatures are from the bestiary tradition. See https://digital.bodleian.ox.ac.uk /objects/a43be554-c5b0-42f0-94e0-70222bb2a964/.

[116] Mittman and Kim, *Inconceivable Beasts*, 85–101.

woman at the bottom of folio 105v.[117] Strikingly, the Conopenas, a type of Cynocephalus (dog-headed creature), on folio 80r of Tiberius B.v is naked, while his counterpart on folio 100r of Vitellius A.xv wears the crimson and blue robes of a king – the same colours worn by King Edgar in the frontispiece of the 966 New Minster Charter (London, BL, Cotton MS Vespasian A.xviii, fol. 2v). Moreover, the Vitellius Conopenas holds an orb in his left hand and a sceptre in his right. His cloak is secured at the shoulder by a rectangular clasp, much like the Sutton Hoo shoulder-clasp in shape and painted yellow, as is the orb, to represent gold.[118] Both his dress and the objects he carries mark him as a king or a creature who performs as a king. The text, however, makes it quite clear that he is a beast, not a human.

> Eac swylce þær beoð cende healfhundingas þa syndon hatene conopenas hy habbað horses mana 7 eafores tuxas 7 hunda heafdu 7 heora oroð bið swylce fyres leg. Þas land beoð neah þæm burgum þe beoð eallum worldwelum gefylled þa is on þa suð healfe egyptana landes.

> [And likewise half-hounds are born there who are called conopenas. They have horses' manes and boars' tusks and dogs' heads and their breath is like a fire's flame. This land is near the cities that are filled with all worldly wealth, that is on the south half of the land of Egypt.]

The style of the Vitellius *Wonders* has been labelled crude, but Asa Simon Mittman and Susan Kim have argued that this is not the case and detailed the ways in which the images work to bring out specific elements of the text and/or nature of the wonders.[119] Moreover, in the context of this manuscript the human ornaments given to the wonders and the elaborate dress of the Conopenas can be understood as examples of the instability of being that permeate the other four texts of the Nowell Codex. In the *Passio of St Christopher* a dog-headed Cynocephalus becomes a saint, while in the *Letter of Alexander the Great to Aristotle* Alexander blunders through India like a monster, killing or looting everything in his path. In *Beowulf* the courts of Heorot and the Grendelkin mirror each other, with Heorot a centre of colonisation doomed to destruction, and in *Judith* the prince Holofernes is a heathen-hound whose attributes of greed and violence Judith may begin to assume as she takes possession of his armour and treasure. What is important to note here, however, is that, in the art of this period, dress and adornment became more than just a sign of status and identity in the everyday lives of men and women: they could also be used to manipulate a reading of a narrative in a certain way. It is unclear whether the depiction of the Conopenas in the Vitellius *Wonders* was meant

---

[117] For a discussion of this image, see Karkov, *Imagining Anglo-Saxon England*, 153–4.

[118] Mittman and Kim, *Inconceivable Beasts*, 17–18; Karkov, *Imagining Anglo-Saxon England*, 106.

[119] Mittman and Kim, *Inconceivable Beasts*.

to suggest that even beasts could be kings, or whether it was meant to suggest that all kings are beasts, or whether all the images of the wonders question identity as something that one can put on or take off like the armour of the fabulated warriors discussed. Whatever the case, by the end of the first millennium English artists were perfectly capable of using visual details and discrepancies or gaps between images and the words they accompanied to create ambiguities, alternative readings, or counter-narratives or even to subvert established traditions or ideas. This ability is a well-known attribute of the designer(s) of the far more famous Bayeux Tapestry (more correctly referred to as the Bayeux Embroidery),[120] unlike the Vitellius *Wonders*, considered an artistic masterpiece, that I will discuss in the next section.

4 The Hand of the Artist

The names of only a small number of artists are known from pre-Norman England, usually from the inscriptions that they left on the works they created. A section of gold foil on the late-seventh-century Harford Farm disc brooch (Norwich Castle Museum) was repaired by a craftsman who added a runic inscription on the back stating that 'Luda repaired this brooch'. The eleventh-century Brussels Reliquary Cross bears the inscription 'Drahmal me worhte' ('Drahmal made me'), and the tenth- or eleventh-century Pershore censer cover is inscribed 'Godric me worhte' ('Godric made me'). Such inscriptions may be advertisements for a metalsmith's work and/or a record of an act of piety.[121] Documentary sources record the names of other artists. Boniface wrote Abbess Eadburg requesting that the nuns of Thanet provide him with a copy of the Epistles of Peter written in gold. He did not mention images, but miniatures and letters were produced with the same tools and often by the same people. Eadfrith was scribe/artist of the Lindisfarne Gospels, in which the illuminated initials and incipits reveal that, from the beginning of English manuscript production, word and image were often inseparable. The terms used for creating words and images could also be the same. The portrait of St Matthew with symbols of the other evangelists on folio 5v of the eighth-century Trier Gospels (Trier, Domschatz cod. 61) is signed 'Thomas scribsit'. Thomas signs on both folios 11r and 125v as one of the scribes who produced the manuscript's text, so it is likely that his signature on folio 5v indicates his production of the image. Conversely, in the early-ninth-century *De Abbatibus*, Æthelwulf wrote of a scribe 'pingere ... uerba'.[122] Godeman, the scribe of the tenth-century Benedictional of St Æthelwold, could also have been an illuminator or at least have had a hand in the manuscript's illumination. Eadui Basan (Eadui the Fat) is thought to have been the

---

[120] On the use of 'tapestry' versus 'embroidery', see Caviness, 'Anglo-Saxon Women'.

[121] See Coatsworth and Pinder, *Anglo-Saxon Goldsmith*, 80.

[122] Dodwell, *Anglo-Saxon Art*, 55–6, notes 82, 83.

artist of some of the miniatures in the manuscripts in which he appears as scribe – the miniature of Benedict with the monks of Canterbury may be his work, as the image's inscriptions are in his hand, and the monk at Benedict's feet is so different from the rest of the monks depicted that it is believed to be a self-portrait.[123] He may also have been the artist of the Hannover/Eadui Gospels in which the four evangelist portraits document the scribal (or artistic) process, from preparing the pen to displaying the finished book.[124]

Evidence of itinerant illuminators may appear in the tenth century.[125] This remains debatable, but it is indisputable that the hands of some scribes and artists are visible in manuscripts attributed to different houses, although this could mean that monks moved or were lent to other monasteries for specific projects rather than that they were itinerant illuminators. The period also saw an increase in diverse and individual styles in all media – like the different styles of the Vitellius and Tiberius versions of the *Wonders of the East*. The precise geometry and lines of the Lindisfarne Gospels reveal nothing of the eccentricities of an individual hand like those of the artists who produced the drawings in either of the two copies of the *Wonders*, because this copy of the Gospels, as the colophon states, was made for God and St Cuthbert, and individual expression was considered an act of vanity.[126] The *Beowulf* manuscript, however, contains poems and wonder tales and could well have been made for a secular patron, while Tiberius B.v is a pseudo-scientific miscellany. The meticulously carved designs and classicising figures of the eighth-century Bewcastle Cross do not reveal the individual hand of the artist in the way that the more imperfectly laid out and executed designs and images, or the puzzling compositions of the tenth-century Leeds or Dearham Crosses (Figures 4 and 9), do.[127] However, for much of the Middle Ages the patrons of art or architecture were considered to be as much responsible for the creation as the artist was, if not more so. The Alfred Jewel states that Alfred ordered it to be made, and the Bewcastle Cross inscription states that Hwætred and another man erected it in memory of one or more people because they were the ones considered central to the meaning and function of the works, not the artists who physically made them. The sculptor Lyl's name appears on a ninth-century cross at Urswick (Lancashire); however, the names of sculptors and masons are largely unrecorded, possibly because sculpture and architecture in particular were credited to patrons rather than artists. The life of Wilfrid details the marvellous architecture and fittings of Ripon and Hexham but

---

[123] Pfaff, 'Eadui Basan'.   [124] Karkov, 'Writing and Having Written'.

[125] Gameson, 'An Itinerant English Master'.

[126] Chapter 57 of the Rule of St Benedict states that demonstrations of pride in artistic skill required artists be removed from their work until they humbled themselves and received permission to return to it: see www.gutenberg.org/ebooks/50040.

[127] Karkov and Treharne, 'Presence of the Hands'.

attributes them to Bishop Wilfrid rather than to his masons. Moreover, most works of early medieval art were produced by workshops – like the Brompton (North Yorkshire) workshop of sculptors responsible for a series of hogbacks and other monuments in the early tenth century, or by teams like the four men who created the Lindisfarne Gospels.

Metalwork

Metalwork was amongst the most valued forms of art due to the precious materials used. In early England, evidence of metalworking exists from a variety of settings and settlement types, including monasteries and estates or courts, and metalsmiths were noteworthy enough to be referred to in the poems *The Fortunes of Men* (line 73a) and *The Gifts of Men* (lines 58–9), while the legendary smith Weland appears in several texts and placenames. In their study of early English goldsmiths, Coatsworth and Pinder note that, in the fifth to early eighth centuries, most evidence for fine metalworking comes from the graves of the metalworkers, but that a sixth-century square-headed brooch mould found at Mucking, Essex, and a fifth-century gold coin with a jeweller's rouge stuck to it from Canterbury indicate that work-shops existed in both villages and high-status settlements like Canterbury.[128] There is also evidence for metalworking of all types within monasteries. Fragments of seventh- or early-eighth-century moulds were uncovered at Hartlepool, a double monastery. The archaeological evidence came from the women's section of the monastery,[129] indicating that women were involved in the art, though it's not clear in what capacity. Metalworking evidence has also come from many other monastic sites including Whitby, Wearmouth-Jarrow, and Lindisfarne.

During the eighth and ninth centuries, metalworking remains are found in increasing numbers in towns, especially important trading towns such as York and Hamwic (Southampton), and at rural settlements and estates including Brandon, Suffolk, and Flixborough, Lincolnshire. In the tenth and eleventh centuries, most evidence for workshops comes from towns; however, metal-working did continue on aristocratic and royal estates. A tenth-century crucible for melting gold comes from the estate of Wynflæd at Faccombe (Netherton), Northamptonshire. Wynflæd's will documents that she left a wooden cup decorated with gold to Eadwold so that he could use the gold to enlarge his arm-ring ('þæt he ice his beah mid þæm golde').[130]

Some goldsmiths had elite status. Dunstan, abbot of Glastonbury (later archbishop of Canterbury and saint), Manning, abbot of Evesham, and

---

[128] Coatsworth and Pinder, *Anglo-Saxon Goldsmith*, 21, 38.

[129] Daniels, 'Anglo-Saxon Monastery at Church Close'.

[130] Coatsworth and Pinder, *Anglo-Saxon Goldsmith*, 22 n.5, 65 n.3, 211.

Spearhafoc, abbot of Abingdon, were all metalworkers as well as artists in other media.[131] Dunstan was goldsmith, scribe, painter, and, possibly, textile worker – though the portrait of him kneeling before Christ in his Classbook (Oxford, Bodleian Library, Auct. F.4.32 fol. 1r) is not by his hand. The Chronicle of the abbots of Evesham describes Manning as a scribe, painter, and goldsmith and records a workshop of secular artists (*artificiosi*) at Evesham under the direction of the master Goderic.[132] Spearhafoc, described as a painter and goldsmith, created large statues of Letard and Queen Bertha for Letard's tomb at Canterbury and was commissioned to make a crown for Edward the Confessor (although he fled the country with the gold and jewels for it).[133] The link between manuscript art and metalworking is not surprising, as tools such as compasses and rulers were used in designing both pages and precious objects; both shared motifs; and both involved small-scale work and attention to fine detail, as the intricacy of surviving fine metalwork indicates. Gold and silver were also used in the writing and illumination of luxury manuscripts.

Some goldsmiths – especially those attached to estates, perhaps also to monastic workshops – were not free. In the tenth-century will of Æthelgifu, the goldsmith Mann was freed with his family and perhaps also his assistant.[134] Others, while free, were hardly amongst the elite. Documentation of changes to smiths' status and references to their travel or work for different patrons indicates that many may have been itinerant. Alternatively, they may simply have changed workshops or patrons as their circumstances changed. English goldsmiths are also known to have worked on the Continent. The eighth-century Tassilo chalice was likely made by an English goldsmith working in Bavaria. Whatever their status, smiths were considered professional artists by the tenth century. Even an elite smith like Spearhafoc worked for both monastic and lay patrons on commission, and the fact that he fled the country with the king's gold and jewels suggests that he didn't consider the church his primary profession. Indeed, Spearhafoc may have used his artistic talents to seek the king's favour along with the wealth and prestige associated with high ecclesiastical office.[135]

Textiles

The production of luxury textiles is aligned with that of metalwork, as gold and precious stones were used in weaving, embroidering, and embellishing textiles for elite patrons. It is impossible to speak of the visibility of artists' hands when it

---

[131] Coatsworth and Pinder, *Anglo-Saxon Goldsmith*, 208–19.

[132] Dodwell, *Anglo-Saxon Art*, 258 n.37, 66.

[133] Coatsworth and Pinder, *Anglo-Saxon Goldsmith*, 209 n.14, n.15.

[134] Coatsworth and Pinder, *Anglo-Saxon Goldsmith*, 213 n.40.

[135] Dodwell, *Anglo-Saxon Art*, 46–7.

comes to textiles as so few survive, and those that do were most likely workshop productions, but early medieval England was especially renowned for particular types of textiles, and these can be considered characteristic of English hands.

Luxury silks were imported from Rome, Byzantium, and beyond from an early date. In addition to the vestments made in tenth-century Winchester especially for the shrine of St Cuthbert, Cuthbert's coffin contained a seventh-century silk from Byzantium decorated with a nature goddess motif, an eighth- or ninth-century Byzantine silk known as the 'Earth and Ocean' silk, and the tenth- or eleventh-century 'Rider' silk which may have been imported from Persia.[136] Some imported silks were reworked or repurposed, and many were no doubt passed on as gifts, so the networks through which both finished textiles and raw materials entered England are difficult to pinpoint.

The production of luxury textiles was largely women's work, though it was never exclusively so. St Dunstan, for example, supplied figural designs for a stole,[137] indicating a role and interest in textile production even if the stole was not actually made with his own hands. However, England was most renowned for its needle-women and especially for their embroidery. The *Liber Eliensis* records that Æthelthryth of Ely embroidered a stole and maniple with gold and precious jewels for St Cuthbert with her own hands.[138] Goscelin wrote that Edith of Wilton was skilled at painting, writing, and music but especially at needlework:

> She embroidered with flowers the pontifical vestments of Christ with all her skill and capacity to make splendid. Here purple, dyed with Punic red, with murex and Sidonian shellfish, and twice dipped scarlet ... were interwoven with gold; chrysolite, topaz, onyx and beryl and precious stones were inter-twined with gold; union pearls, the shells' treasure, which only India pro-duces in the east and Britain, the land of the English in the west, were set like the stars in gold; the golden insignia of the cross, the golden images of the saints were outlined with a surround of pearls.[139]

The description is exaggerated and laced with biblical allusions, but on a general level it accords with surviving examples of luxury ecclesiastical textiles. Goscelin praised English women generally for the high quality of their embroidery and especially for the fabrics that they decorated with gold-work and precious stones.[140] Edith also had a fondness for dressing in rich apparel, wearing purple over her hair shirt, for which she was criticised by the bishop, and keeping a chest full of fine clothes.[141]

---

[136] Owen-Crocker, *Dress in Anglo-Saxon England*, 299 n.35
[137] Dodwell, *Anglo-Saxon Art*, 39.   [138] Fairweather, *Liber Eliensis*, 30.
[139] Wright and Loncar, 'Vita of Edith', 38.   [140] Dodwell, *Anglo-Saxon Art*, 45, 57.
[141] Wright and Loncar, 'Vita of Edith', 40, 42–3.

Queen Edith, wife of Edward the Confessor, was also a renowned embroiderer, clothing Edward in silks, gold, and jewels, including gold ornaments made by smiths working to her requirements.

> In the ornamentation of these no count was made of the cost of the precious stones, rare gems and shining pearls that were used. As regards mantles, tunics, boots and shoes, the amount of gold which flowed in the various complicated floral designs was not weighed. The throne, adorned with coverings embroidered with gold, gleamed in every part ... His saddle and horse-trappings were hung with little beasts and birds made from gold by smiths under her direction.[142]

Professional embroiderers are identified in various documentary sources. A woman named Leofgyth worked for the court both before and after 1066, and shortly after the Conquest a woman named Ælfgyth was employed by the sheriff of Buckinghamshire to teach his daughter to embroider with gold.[143]

Two sets of ecclesiastical textiles embroidered with gold and other substances survive. The earliest are the late-eighth- or early-ninth-century Maaseik embroideries known as the *casula* of saints Harlindis and Relindis. The *casula* consists of a number of pieces of embroidery worked in coloured silk on a linen background in a southern English style. They are decorated with embroidered arcading filled with zoomorphic, foliate, and geometric ornament worked in multicoloured silk and gold threads. They include painted cloth and metalwork appliqués, and there is evidence of pearls having been sewn onto the arcades and roundels that enclose the decoration, although these may not have been part of the original fabric.[144] The incorporation of metalwork and painting into textiles was likely more common than is thought given the number of artists working in multiple media recorded in the documentary sources.

The stole, maniple, and "girdle" from St Cuthbert's coffin were made in southern England between 909 and 916. Inscriptions embroidered on the stole and maniple state that they were made for Frithestan, bishop of Winchester, on the order of Queen Ælfflæd, wife of Edward the Elder. They were probably presented to Cuthbert's shrine in 934 by Edward's son Æthelstan. The embroideries are worked in gold and coloured silks on a woven silk background and are important as surviving examples of a major art form now largely lost to us – and because their figural and foliate ornament are early examples of the so-called 'Winchester Style' that would become popular throughout England in the second half of the tenth century. The style, which will be discussed in

---

[142] Barlow, *Life of King Edward*, 24–5.   [143] Dodwell, *Anglo-Saxon Art*, 70, 72, 78.
[144] See further Budny and Tweddle, 'Maaseik Embroideries'.

more detail, is characterised by lush acanthus ornament, rich colours, and, in manuscript illumination, lavish gold borders filled with acanthus ornament that expands across and through the bars of the borders as if they were a trellis. Documentary sources reveal that elaborate vestments and altar cloths like the Cuthbert embroideries were popular gifts and bequests throughout early medieval England. In the eighth century the altars at Ripon and Hexham were covered with silk decorated with gold,[145] while Æthelwulf's *De Abbatibus* (written 803–21) describes wall-hangings at Lindisfarne that depicted the miracles of Christ and were worked in glowing red metal – presumably gold.[146] In the tenth and eleventh centuries, King Edgar gave gold-embroidered cloaks to Ely and Glastonbury, a woman named Wulfwaru willed a set of mass-vestments to Bath Abbey, and Alfwaru left an alb and chasuble, wall-hangings, and a richly decorated cushion seat to Ramsey Abbey.[147]

The c.1080 Bayeux Embroidery is the only surviving early medieval English wall-hanging, but sources indicate that this type of artwork was a common form of religious and secular decoration. The hangings left by Alfwaru to Ramsey Abbey, along with those given to the Cuthbert community by King Æthelstan and the hanging worked with scenes from the life of Byrhtnoth (hero of the Battle of Maldon) given to Ely by his widow Ælfflæd, may all have been in secular use before they were bequeathed to the church. Like these, the Embroidery is undoubtedly and primarily the work of English needlewomen, even if men might have been involved in some capacity.[148] The Bayeux Embroidery is less elaborate than the *casula* of Harlindis and Relindis or the Cuthbert embroideries. It is worked in wool thread on a linen background, but its length (68.4 m) and narrative detail make up for the humbler materials used. While there is no proof, the Embroidery is thought to have been made for Bishop Odo of Bayeux, probably for a secular hall. The Embroidery details the events leading up to the Norman conquest of England, with the missing final portion believed to have depicted William enthroned, balancing the image of Edward the Confessor enthroned with which it begins. It is not clear, however, that the Embroidery was meant as a celebration of the Norman victory. The artists have not guided the viewer to either a pro- or anti-Norman stance; instead, they created a work that allows viewers to put together the different parts of the composition – the main visual narrative, the border images, and the textual labels that accompany but do not explain most scenes – to create different interpretations of or commentaries on the events depicted. How the

---

[145] Colgrave, *Life of Bishop Wilfrid*, 37, 47, 121.   [146] Campbell, *De Abbatibus*, lines 633–5.

[147] Dodwell, *Anglo-Saxon Art*, 23.

[148] See Caviness, 'Anglo-Saxon Women', for a discussion of the Embroidery and the gendering of the terms 'tapestry' and 'embroidery' in scholarship.

scene of a woman standing in a doorway with a man reaching for her cheek in the main panel, the images of two naked men in the border beneath them, and the inscription 'Ubi unus clericus et Ælfgyva' ('Here a cleric and Ælfgyva') are meant to be interpreted remains a matter of debate. Who is the cleric? Is the reference to the English queen Ælfgyfu/Emma? But she was of Norman birth. In other words, one could read the Embroidery as either pro-Norman or pro-English, depending on how one put the different elements together. This is typical of much English art of the late tenth and eleventh centuries and may reflect the problematic and divisive reigns of rulers from Æthelred II through to William the Conqueror.[149]

Manuscript Illumination

As indicated, some goldsmiths were also scribes and/or illuminators of manuscripts, and images like that of the monk – possibly Eadui Basan – at the feet of St Benedict in the Eadui Psalter (Figure 7) may be self-portraits. While there is no way to be certain that the image is a self-portrait, the details of the stubbly chin and girth of the monk suggest an individuality that is in keeping with the idea of a portrait. The other images of reading or writing monks that fill the pages of early medieval English manuscripts may also be portraits or self-portraits. While we do not know their names, individual illuminators' hands are often recognisable in the same way that scribes' are. The hand of the artist of the Ramsey Psalter (London, BL, Harley MS 2904), produced c.975–1000, possibly in Winchester but more likely in Ramsey, has also been identified in the c.1000 Boulogne Gospels (Boulogne, Bibliothèque Municipale MS 11) attributed to Saint-Bertin. The attribution of the manuscripts to different houses on both sides of the English Channel might indicate that this artist was itinerant,[150] although his mastery of drawing may simply have meant that he was a monk who either changed houses or whose talents were in great demand. The Crucifixion on folio 3v of the Ramsey Psalter (Figure 14) both is iconographically complex and demonstrates an impressive ability to manipulate line and form in order to convey motion and emotion, making it one of the period's great surviving works of art.[151] While not as admired as the Ramsey Psalter Crucifixion, the images of the Boulogne Gospel exhibit the same expressive forms and facial expressions as well as some of the same delicacy and variety of lines. For the most part, however, illuminators tended to work in the styles that were popular in a given region or period, making individual hands difficult to

---

[149] Karkov, 'Conquest and Material Culture'.

[150] He also worked on Orléans, Bibliothèque Municipale MS 175, attributed to Fleury.

[151] Karkov, *Art of Anglo-Saxon England*, 196–9; Heslop, 'The Implication of the Utrecht Psalter', 273; online at www.bl.uk/collection-items/ramsey-psalter.

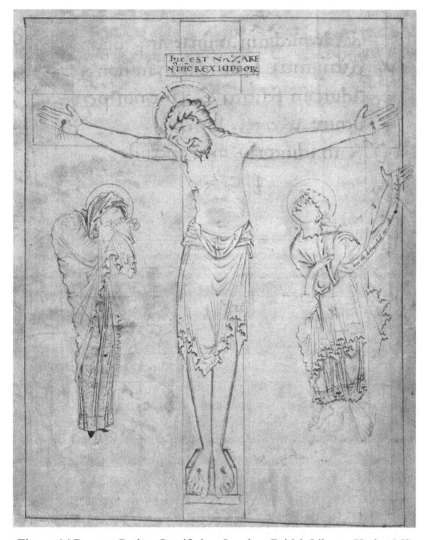

Figure 14 Ramsey Psalter Crucifixion, London, British Library, Harley MS 2904, fol. 3v. Wikimedia Commons/public domain.

distinguish unless specific forms of line or details of images are repeated from manuscript to manuscript.

The styles of early medieval English art are defined geographically. Art historians write about the Insular or Hiberno-Saxon style of the seventh–eighth centuries, popular in northern Britain and Ireland and exemplified by the Lindisfarne Gospels (Figure 6), or the Mercian Style of the eighth–ninth centuries. However, these classifications include art in all media, not just manuscripts. There are also sub-styles. The 'Tiberius' group of manuscripts is formed by a number of books produced south of the Humber in Mercia, Kent, and Wessex during the eighth and ninth centuries. It includes manuscripts attributed to Canterbury and/or nearby monasteries such as Minster-in-Thanet, as well as Mercian houses.[152] The group is united by its classicising figure style and a distinctive naturalistic style of animal ornament, with energetically posed beasts contained in discrete compartments and long-necked biting beasts, the latter often forming initials or parts of initials.[153] Michelle Brown proposed that three of the group's manuscripts (Harley 7653, Harley 2965, and Royal 2.A.xx) were made or owned by women and suggested further that either of or both the Vespasian Psalter and the Stockholm Codex Aureus (Figures 2 and 3) had been produced at the double monastery of Minster-in-Thanet.[154] While there is no proof of the production of luxury manuscripts at Minster-in-Thanet, there is also no reason to believe that such manuscripts could not have been produced there. Brown's point is that we shouldn't assume that all manuscripts were the product of big-name male communities like Canterbury unless otherwise proven. As is the case with the majority of the period's manuscripts, the hands of individual scribes have been identified, but not those of individual illuminators, so that for the latter we can generally speak only of schools of illumination. Adding to the difficulty of identifying individual illuminators is the fact that illuminations can rarely be dissected into individual repeated pen strokes in the same way that letters can, as well as the possibility that an image could be the work of more than one artist. Even manuscripts as close stylistically as the Codex Aureus and the Vespasian Psalter show subtle differences in style – the use of line or shading and highlighting – when examined closely.

The two named, or rather misnamed, styles of tenth- and eleventh-century illumination – the 'Winchester Style' and the style of outline drawing once known as the 'Canterbury Style' – include manuscripts that actually exhibit

---

[152] London, BL, Cotton MS Vespasian A.i (Vespasian Psalter), eighth century; Stockholm, Kungliga Biblioteket, MS A.135 (Stockholm Codex Aureus), mid-eighth century; London, BL, Cotton MS Tiberius C.ii (Bede's *Historia ecclesiastica*), eighth–ninth century; C.C.C.C., MS 69 (Gregory the Great, Homilae), eighth–ninth century; C.C.C.C. MS 144 (Corpus Glossary), early ninth century; London, BL, Royal MS 1.E.vi (Royal Bible), 800–50; Vatican, Bibl. Apost., Barb. lat. 570 (Barbarini Gospels), late eighth century; London, BL, Harley MS 7653 (prayerbook), late eight–early ninth century; Oxford, Bodleian Library Hatton 93 (Commentary on the Mass), eighth–ninth century; St Petersburg, State Library, Cod. F.v.1.8 (St Petersburg Gospels), c.800; London, BL, Royal MS 2.A.xx (Royal prayerbook), 800–25; London, BL, Harley MS 2965 (Book of Nunnaminster), 800–25; Cambridge, University Library, MS Ll.1.10 (Book of Cerne), c.820–40.

[153] On the Tiberius Group, see Brown, 'Mercian Manuscripts?'.

[154] Brown, 'Female Book-Ownership'.

a wide range of and combinations of styles. In both cases, the names conform to Brown's criticism of assigning manuscripts to groups identified solely with the most prominent male monastic and ecclesiastical centres; and manuscripts illuminated using the techniques and motifs used to distinguish these styles were produced across the country and not just in the areas around Winchester and Canterbury. That said, the Winchester Style gets its name from the fact that some of the most famous of its manuscripts are identified with figures or events clearly connected to Winchester, like the New Minster Charter or the Benedictional of St Æthelwold. However, the style also appears in luxury manuscripts not associated with either the court or church at Winchester, like the Ramsey Psalter. The great initial B of Psalm 1 (Figure 15) displays the golden barred borders and acanthus ornament characteristic of the 'Winchester' style, but the Crucifixion miniature that faces it is in the outline drawing technique associated with the style of Canterbury manuscripts such as the Harley 603 Psalter (London, BL, Harley MS 603), and, as noted already, its artist also worked in Saint Bertin and Fleury. Admittedly, it has been suggested that the Ramsey Psalter is indeed a Winchester manuscript, but the Crucifixion is not in the Winchester style. The main features identified with Winchester manuscripts are the fleshy acanthus ornament that often wraps itself around the gilded trellis-like frames, the extensive use of gold, and the richly coloured figures whose faces and forms are modelled from layers of coloured-ink wash, but, in the image of the monks of Canterbury and St Benedict in the Eadui Psalter, this figure style is combined with the outline drawing style more commonly associated with the 'Canterbury' school of illumination.

Drawing, wherever it was produced, was a major art form in tenth- and eleventh-century England. It was far more popular in England than anywhere else in Europe at the time, and this is especially true of coloured outline drawing. In 1952, Francis Wormald was struck by the 'extremely calligraphic' nature of the English drawing style,[155] while more recently Melanie Holcomb has discussed both the sophisticated use of drawing in England from as early as the late ninth century and the profound influence drawings from early medieval England were to have on post-Conquest art on both sides of the Channel.[156] A wide range of individual hands and drawing techniques is evident within the corpus of tenth- and eleventh-century English drawings. The firm lines of the drawing of St Dunstan at the feet of Christ, for example, contrast markedly with the flickering energy and variety of pen strokes seen in the Ramsey Psalter Crucifixion.

---

[155] Wormald, *English Drawings*, 31, 55–6.   [156] Holcomb, 'Strokes of Genius'.

Figure 15 Ramsey Psalter initial to Psalm 1, London, British Library, Harley
MS 2904, fol. 4r. Wikimedia Commons/public domain.

The Harley 603 Psalter (London, BL, Harley MS 603)[157] is an appropriate
work with which to end this section for a number of reasons: the creative way in
which its artists made use of specific sources or models disproving the common
notion that medieval artists were mere copyists; its individual artists' hands are

---

[157] See www.bl.uk/manuscripts/FullDisplay.aspx?index=235&ref=Harley_MS_603.

identifiable; it was illuminated over a 100-year period, providing evidence of the ways in which illuminators (and scribes) responded to or accommodated the work of their predecessors; it demonstrates how art could be used to provide subtle commentary on historical or political events.

Harley 603 was begun in the early eleventh century at either St Augustine's or Christ Church, Canterbury. It is a loose copy of, and shows the influence of, the ninth-century Carolingian Utrecht Psalter (Utrecht, Universiteitsbibliotheek, MS 32), which was brought to England shortly before the year 1000. Like Utrecht, each psalm is accompanied by a dynamic pen and ink drawing that provides a 'literal' rendering of the individual words or verses of the psalm. It is not, however, a literal copy of Utrecht. The drawings in Harley 603 are created from a variety of coloured inks rather than the monochrome brown ink of Utrecht, there is great variation in the details copied, others are omitted, some images were significantly altered to incorporate multiple references, a prefatory drawing was added, and inhabited and historiated initials were included throughout Harley. The initials in Utrecht are quite plain. The opening sequence to Psalm 1 is a good example of the way in which the artists remained close to the images in Utrecht but added details that both change the image and are picked up in drawings later in the manuscript. A prefatory miniature depicting the Trinity has been added to Harley 603 (folio 1r), showing God and Christ embracing, their faces pressed close against each other, while the dove of the Holy Spirit whispers into God's ear. A blank scroll unrolls across their bodies and is grasped by the feet of the Holy Spirit, indicating the inseparable nature of the three-in-one and the primacy of the Word. The blessed man on the left-hand side of the drawing in Harley 603 (folio 1v) reads the tiny opening words to Psalm 1 that are written on the pages of the book in front of him, while the same figure in Utrecht is writing in his book, which displays tiny dots and squiggles rather than actual words. In the historiated initial with which the text of the Psalm on the facing page (Figure 16) begins, Christ stands holding an open book and a scroll that unrolls into the hands of an archbishop, most likely Alphege of Canterbury, lying prostrate at his feet. Together the three drawings demonstrate a focus on reading, writing, and understanding the word/Word, as well as the incorporation of figures or events from Canterbury history into the Psalm narratives that are unique. Despite the focus on reading and the Word, however, the eccentric text of the manuscript could actually never have been used; it was intended from the beginning as a display manuscript.

The hands of ten different artists have been identified in the Psalter's drawings, with two of the artists also amongst the manuscript's four scribes. William

Figure 16 Initial to Psalm 1, London, British Library, Harley MS 603, fol. 2r.
Wikimedia Commons/public domain.

Noel has identified the artists by the letters A through J, with scribes D and
E being the artist-scribes.[158] Artists A, B, C, D, and F all worked c.1010–30,
Artist E c.1020–30, Artist G in the 1070s, and Artist H c.1100–1150. Artist
A made the illustrations in the first quire (aside from the Trinity) and those on
folios 9r, 10v, 11r, 11v, 16r, and 16v (all in quire two). Artist B illustrated quires
three and four and added the drawings to folios 12r, 15r, and 17r of quire two.
Artist C made the drawings on folios 13 and 14. Artist D illustrated quire nine.

---

[158] The following description of the artists' work is based on Noel's identifications, *Harley Psalter*,
42–120, 207–13.

Artist F did the drawings in quires ten and eleven and the drawing at the bottom of folio 59r. Artist E completed folio 15v, did the drawings on folios 53r, 58v, 61r, 62v, 67r, 70r, 70v, and 72v, and added most of the rubrics. Artist I provided the miniature of the Trinity that prefaces the Psalter, the *Beatus vir* initial with the prostrate archbishop for Psalm 1, and the initial for Psalm 101 on folio 50r.[159] Artist J did the initials on folios 2r–27v, aside from the *Beatus vir* initial, and folio 54r. Artist G completed the drawings on folio 28 and added a drawing on folio 17v, the initial to Psalm 48, and also added to the work of the earlier artists. Artist H made the drawings on folios 29r–35r, the initials to Psalm 51 on folio 29r, and the initial to Psalms 53 and 57 on folios 29v and 31v.

The manuscript was produced in two phases: an early-eleventh-century phase, during which work proceeded quickly; and a later-eleventh–twelfth century phase, during which work was sporadic.[160] The artists of the second phase imitated, referred back to, and added to the work of the earlier artists in the process of creating their own work. For example, Artist-scribe E copied motifs and stylistic details from the work of earlier Artists A–D and F. His drawing in the text of Psalm 118 on folio 61r is based on that of Artist F's drawing at the beginning of the Psalm.[161] Both Artist-scribe E and Artist G added details to the earlier drawings in order to clarify or update them.[162] Artist I's work on the Trinity miniature and *Beatus vir* initial is unprecedented but expands on the focus on word/Word already established in the earlier phase of production. The Trinity miniature is also an example of the increasing interest in the representation of internal emotion and drama in art that appeared in the late tenth and eleventh centuries.[163]

Perhaps most notable for its content is the work of the twelfth-century Artist H, who borrowed details of the style and content of some of his drawings from Artists G and I, while at the same time creating images completely his own. His initial to Psalm 51 and drawing to Psalm 52 (Figure 17) on folio 29r refer back to the image of the archbishop at the feet of Christ in the initial to Psalm 1 by Artist I and the detail of the wicked man in the drawing that introduces Psalm 1 by Artist A, respectively. The archbishop in the Psalm 1 initial is believed to be Archbishop Alphege (1005–12). The man being stoned to death in the illustration to Psalm 52 is believed to be a thinly veiled reference to Alphege's martyrdom by the Danes – he was pelted with bones and then killed with an axe. The image of the evil king above him is based on that of the wicked man at the right of

---

[159] On Artist I's work, see Karkov, 'Reading the Trinity'.   [160] Noel, *Harley Psalter*, 186.

[161] Noel, *Harley Psalter*, 89.   [162] Gameson, 'The Anglo-Saxon Artists'.

[163] Karkov, 'Reading the Trinity'; Raw, *Trinity and Incarnation*, 15–18.

Figure 17 Illustration of Psalm 52. © The British Library Board, London, British Library, Harley MS 603, fol. 29r.

the drawing for Psalm 1 and has been interpreted as an anti-military message against Cnut or his father Svein, who was responsible for Alphege's martyrdom.[164] The drawing served as model for the twelfth-century St Alphege (Ælfheah) window in Canterbury Cathedral[165] and may have served as a veiled warning against any contemporary interference with the independence or wealth of the monastery by the Normans.[166]

---

[164] Chazelle, 'Violence and the Virtuous Ruler', 341; Karkov, 'Conquest and Material Culture', 191–2.
[165] Noel, *Harley Psalter*, 101.   [166] Karkov, 'Conquest and Material Culture', 191–2.

The Harley Psalter is all about Canterbury history, devotional life, and manuscript culture. Its artists were in many ways faithful to their original Utrecht model, but they also departed from it so as to both centre their Canterbury community of readers and express their individuality as artists. Harley 603 was ultimately left unfinished, perhaps when the c.1155–60 Eadwine Psalter (Cambridge, Trinity College, MS R.17.1), which is even more explicitly about Canterbury, was begun.[167] The great portrait of the scribe Eadwine (who may also have been an artist) in conversation with the letters of the book he has just created on folio 283v of that manuscript is a demonstration of how the English interest in speaking objects and visual documentation of the processes of manuscript production continued to develop into the Romanesque period, as well as the more prominent position both artists and scribes would enjoy in the art of the later Middle Ages.

5 Looking Back at Early Medieval England

The formation of England did not end with the unification of the various kingdoms that had been established on the island prior to the Norman Conquest; indeed, England is still in formation. This final section looks back at how England saw itself immediately pre- and post-Conquest and how that image has been perceived from places outside of and times beyond early medieval England.

In addition to the *Wonders of the East*, the Tiberius B.v manuscript contains the famous Cotton world map (Figure 18), which depicts a world in which the island of Britain is simultaneously set apart from the rest of the world yet expands out to create a world in its own image. Britain/England is the angular shape in the lower left corner, with only Ireland and Thule beyond it. Set apart though it might be, its shape is repeated in increasingly larger form in the land mass of Europe just above it and in the much larger shape consisting of Africa, India, the Middle East, Asia Minor, and Asia beyond that. It is a fantasy of England as a 'repeating island', in Elizabeth DeLoughrey's development of the term, an island that eerily foreshadows its own colonial reproduction. DeLoughrey refers specifically to modern England's repeating itself in the island colonies of the British Empire. The geography of the Cotton map uncannily foreshadows that process, and DeLoughrey traces the roots of the island's imperial repetition back to its colonisation by the Angles and Saxons.[168] The Cotton map also presents the island as hovering between past and present. It is

---

[167] See https://mss-cat.trin.cam.ac.uk/viewpage.php?index=1229.

[168] DeLoughrey, *Routes and Roots*, 7. Antonio Benítez-Rojo coined the term 'repeating island' to describe a more positive image of the expansion of island culture outward from the Caribbean as migrants carried their home cultures across the globe: Benítez-Rojo, *The Repeating Island*.

Figure 18 Cotton world map, London, British Library, Cotton MS Tiberius B.v.,
fol. 56v. Wikimedia Commons/public domain.

labelled Britannia, its Roman name, which had a fluid meaning, sometimes
referring to the whole island and sometimes to just a part of it, although it came
to be equated specifically with England.[169] The name Britannia enjoyed particular popularity during Elizabethan times, coinciding with the expansion of
England overseas and the beginnings of an Empire,[170] in which England forced
its image onto much of the world, perhaps even more effectively than had the

---

[169] Davies, *First English Empire*, 31–53; McColl, 'Meaning of "Britain"', 248–69.
[170] Hewitt, 'Britannia (fl. 1st–21st cent.)'.

Romans. Both that earlier Roman empire and the history, language, and art of early medieval England would have profound roles to play in the images and practices of the British Empire and the nationalism and racism that went along with it.

The English had imagined themselves as exceptional since the age of Bede, both isolated at the edge of the world and central to it, welcoming and assimilating some cultures, expelling or isolating others. Bede documents the assimilation of and violence towards the Britons, a scenario backed up by the archaeological evidence.[171] Seemingly more welcoming, the prologue to the laws of King Alfred stipulated that '[u]tan cumene and elðeodige ne geswenc, ðu no, forðon ðe ge wæron giu elðeodige on Egipta londe' ('you shall not oppress foreigners and strangers because you were once strangers in the land of Egypt'),[172] but its phrasing sets the English above other peoples by repeating the Exodus myth of a chosen people. Given these attitudes towards internal and external strangers and the focus on English and Englishness expressed by Alfred and his successors, it is ironic that the name Britannia by which the island is known on the Cotton map and through later history originates from the Welsh/Brittonic name for the island *Prytanī*, the Welsh having been amongst the first to be segregated during the early medieval period. On the map Wales is labelled *Morenwergas*, which could be translated as Morgannwg (Glamorgan)[173] or as a place of criminals or monsters (*mor-wearg/werg* meaning criminal, monster, evil spirit),[174] moor-dwellers,[175] or 'wild men of the moors'.[176] On the other hand, across the Channel, Brittany and Normandy are labelled *Suðbrytta* (South Britain), so, if the map dates from late in the second quarter of the eleventh century, the choice of Britannia rather than England may reflect growing Norman interest in the island and a claim to it that circumvents Englishness and presages the coming of a new empire.

In Norman England, the pre-Conquest past became a problematic area, a period with which the new rulers desired to establish continuity, hence bolstering their legitimacy, but one needing to be kept distant enough that the past did not become a rallying point for English nationalists. This is seen in the material record surrounding Durham Cathedral, where the new structure and its smaller copies at Lindisfarne and Dunfermline employed a new style of architecture but one that retained some features from the earlier period. The copies of the cathedral also established links between the reformed Cuthbert community at Durham, their original home at Lindisfarne, and the seat of their most powerful patrons, Malcolm and Margaret of Scotland. Margaret was a direct descendent of King Alfred, and when her daughter, Edith/Matilda, married

---

[171] See Section 1.   [172] Gates, 'Prologue', translation my own.

[173] Foys, Wacha, et al., 'Morgenwergas',   [174] Karkov, *Imagining Anglo-Saxon England*, 70.

[175] Naismith, https://twitter.com/rory_naismith/status/973146027736825856?lang=en.

[176] McGuigan, 'Neither Scotland nor England', 110.

Henry I in 1100 the bond between the old West Saxon royal line and the new Norman one was cemented.

I have described a certain ambivalence in the art of the period, especially at places like Dunfermline, where Malcolm and Margaret alternated in their support for either the English or the Normans depending on political expediency. The past, no matter how heavily reworked or rewritten, could not be buried and continued to haunt. This is documented by the chroniclers Symeon of Durham, William of Malmesbury, Henry of Huntingdon, and Geoffrey of Monmouth, all of whom rewrote the past and its continuity with the present in very different ways. The past also persists in poems such as *Durham* and *The Grave*. In *Durham*, the city with its cathedral becomes a kind of island paradise surrounded by a river full of fish and woods abounding in game but inhabited only by the dead.

> Is in ðere byri eac   bearnum gecyðed
>
> ðe arfesta   eadig Cudberch
>
> and ðes clene   cyninges heafud,
>
> Osuualdes, Engle leo,   and Aidan bsicop,
>
> Eadberch and Eadfirð   æðele geferes.
>
> Is ðer inne midd heom   Æðelwold biscop
>
> and breoma bocera Beda,   and Boisil abbot,
>
> ðe clene Cudberte   on gecheðe
>
> lerde lustum,   and he his lara well genom.
>
> Eardiæð æt ðem eadige   in in ðem minstre
>
> unarimede   reliquia,
>
> ðær monia wundrum gewurðað   ðæs ðe writ seggeð,
>
> midd ðene drihnes wer   domes bideð.
>
>   (lines 9–21)

[There is also in the city, as it is known to men, the righteous blessed Cuthbert and the head of the pure king – Oswald, lion of the English – and Bishop Aidan, Eadbert and Eadfrith, the noble companions. Inside with them is Bishop Æthelwold and the famous scholar Bede, and Abbot Boisil, who vigorously taught the pure Cuthbert in his youth, and he (i.e., Cuthbert) learned his lessons well. Along with the blessed one, there remain in the minster countless relics where many miracles occur, as it is said in writing, awaiting the Judgement with the man of God.][177]

---

[177] Text and translation Blurton, '*Reliquia*', 40–1.

The poem is preserved only in the late twelfth-century Cambridge, University Library, Ff.1.27, a compilation of historical texts with a focus on Durham and the North.

Marjorie Housley describes *The Grave* as memorialising England as an ever-present lost soul, an eternally decomposing corpse.[178] *The Grave* is preserved on folio 170r of the twelfth-century Oxford, Bodleian Library, Bodley 343, which also contains Old English and Middle English homilies, thus looking to the past while instructing the reader in the present. It is addressed to a living person but one already inhabiting the grave.

> Swa ðu scealt on molde   wunien ful calde,
>
> dimme and deorcæ.   Þet den fulæt on honde.
>
> Dureleas is þet hus   and dearc hit is wiðinnen.
>
> Ðær þu bist feste bidytt   and dæð hefð þa cæge.
>
> Ladlic is þet eorð-hus   and grim inne to wunien.
>
> Ðer þu scealt wunien   and wurmes þe todeleð.
>
> Ðus ðu bist ilegd   and ladæst þine fronden ...[179]
>
> (lines 11–17)

[So you must live, stone cold in the earth. In dimness and darkness that den decays at your hands. Doorless is that house and dark it is within. There you are imprisoned and death has the key. Terrible is that earth house and it is grim to live there. There you must live and worms will share you. Thus you are laid, and you leave your friends ...][180]

The corpse, like the earlier English past, is dead and beyond reach, but at the same time it is physically present, not yet dismembered by worms, and emotionally or psychically present in the memories of the speaker/reader. Rather than maintaining an attachment to the past while discrediting the present,[181] the poem keeps the past encrypted within land and mind, a ghostly presence that could reappear any time. Death in *The Grave* is a traumatic event, in *Durham* a spiritual one, but both present the reader with spectres of the living dead, different but equally haunting images of an early English past that will not die.

Conquest has two sides, one violent and destructive and the other concerned with the preservation of symbols or stories, and this is evident in art no less than in documentary or literary records. The Harley 603 Psalter is one example, the twelfth-century Artist H having incorporated elements of pre-Conquest style and iconography into his own work. Artist H's additions to the Psalter may have

---

[178] Housley, 'Uneasy Presences'.   [179] Text Jones, *Old English Shorter Poems*, 230.
[180] Translation Jones, 'Relining *The Grave*', 76–7.   [181] Housley, 'Uneasy Presences', 437.

been subtle warnings against royal attempts to interfere with the Canterbury monastery in which it was produced. Similar warnings appear in the lavishly illustrated *Life and Miracles of St Edmund King and Martyr* (New York, Pierpont Morgan Library, M.736) made at Bury St Edmunds c.1125–30.[182] Barbara Abou-el-Haj and Cynthia Hahn have shown how images of an earlier past are deployed in the twelfth-century present with the manuscript's depictions of Edmund as a Christ-like figure, the violent acts committed by the Danes and King Svein, and Svein's equally violent death designed as warnings against episcopal and royal attempts to tax and/or interfere with the running of the monastery.[183]

The manuscript is one of an interconnected group of artworks promoting the cult of Edmund and the prominence of Bury St Edmunds c.1070–1130. Edmund was a ninth-century king of East Anglia martyred by the Danes in 869. The monastery was founded in 1020 and enjoyed substantial political and economic privileges, making it amongst the wealthiest of England's monasteries at the Conquest. The manuscript's central texts, a copy of the *passio* of Edmund written by Abbo of Fleury and a copy of the *miracula* of Edmund commissioned by the monastery, promoted Edmund as a king and saint of national importance and the monastery as an international pilgrimage centre whose saint was more powerful than those of Rome or Jerusalem.[184] Edmund has a miraculous ability to protect his community. Originally martyred for refusing to submit to Ingvar and the Danes, his relics go on to work miracles, prominent among them the paralysing of thieves who attack his church (folio 18v) and his appearance before the dying Svein, who had refused the monastery's request for exemption from tribute. Svein's death is illustrated twice in the manuscript, once on folio 21v of the prefatory cycle of full-page miniatures, and again in the historiated initial to the prologue of the *miracula* on folio 23r. In the former, a crowned Edmund materialises to stab Svein in the chest with a spear and retrieve the abbey's payment. Svein dies horribly, his eyes rolled back in his head, tongue sticking out, splayed hands reaching out to either side of his body, and face tinged a deathly grey. In the initial to the prologue Edmund is dressed as a haloed warrior with helmet, spear, and shield, and Svein dies an equally dramatic death. The repetition of the scene across successive manuscript openings indicates its key place in the manuscript's overall message.

Equally important is the manuscript's depiction of England and the relationship it establishes between England past and present. It goes back to the origins of England with the first of the prefatory miniatures, the arrival of the Angles, Saxons, and Jutes on folio 7r (Figure 19). The tribes wear the helmets and tunics and bear the shields of twelfth-century warriors, as do the invading Danes on folio 9v, and indeed Edmund

---

[182] See www.themorgan.org/collection/Life-and-Miracles-of-St-Edmund.

[183] Abou-el-Haj, 'Bury St Edmunds'; Hahn, 'Peregrinatio et Natio'.

[184] Hahn, 'Peregrinatio et Natio', 119, 125.

Figure 19 Angles, Saxons, and Jutes sail to England, New York, Pierpont Morgan Library, MS M.736, fol. 7r. © Getty Images.

in the initial described previously. We should not expect historical accuracy from a twelfth-century artist, but the effect is to suggest that all invaders and all invasions are the same, and that the events of the past are continually capable of being replayed in the present. England itself is a blessed isle. In this first miniature it is a circle floating in a sea full of fish and enclosing verdant trees and fields and a walled city. The island's air and sky are a bright orangish colour articulated with cloud patterns that suggest the heavens and divine light. The image is actually close to that of the verbal description of Durham in the poem *Durham*, save only for the absence of woodland animals. The composition also captures the idea of the island as a special place, set apart from the world yet accessible. The Angles, Saxons, and Jutes approach and surround the island, yet its shores remain intact. The invading troops do eventually land and kill the Britons, who flee or lie dead beneath the feet of the colonisers' horses (folio 7v), and the conquerors divide the island up amongst themselves (folio 8r). Edmund is crowned king on folio 8v. These opening miniatures create an abbreviated narrative of consecutive events that in reality took place centuries apart and in the text of the *passio* are spread across three chapters. As Hahn notes, Edmund was king only of East Anglia, but the opening images conflate the sub-kingdom with the island as a whole, so that Edmund is effectively shown as both king of the whole island and as one of its original colonisers. The sacred nature of Edmund's kingship and/or the inextricable union of his kingly and saintly identities in the promotion of the monastery are underscored visually by the similarity of his pose and dress in the scene of his coronation and in the miniature of his saintly apotheosis on folio 22v, the final image in the prefatory cycle.

Edmund's martyrdom connects him to the land over which he is king. Dressed in a green robe and bound to a leafy fruit-bearing tree, he is mocked and beaten before being shot full of arrows, being beheaded, and having his head hidden in a bush (folios 13r–14v). The lush landscape in which he dies recalls the fertile landscape of the island towards which the Germanic invaders sail in the opening miniature. Admittedly, green is used heavily throughout the cycle, but there can be no doubt that the artist wanted to depict the island as a blessed place and its colonisers as a special people, as part of the miniature of the Danes slaughtering the English on folio 10r is modelled on the massacre of the innocents,[185] recalling the biblical origin legends that Bede and other authors had established for the Angles/English.

The final image of the cycle, the apotheosis of Edmund (Figure 20), refers back to his crowning as king of East Anglia/England. Aside from colour, the shape and details of the garments he wears in the two miniatures are the same. In the first, he receives a sceptre from one of the two bishops who flank him, while in the second he receives a grander gold and jewelled sceptre from one of the two angels who stand in the same position as the bishops. The heavenly crown placed on his head by two angels who sweep down from heaven is the same shape as that in the earlier miniature but grander, with a larger cross and jewelled fillets very like those of a Byzantine-style imperial crown. In both miniatures the king looks directly out at the viewer, commanding attention and placing the viewer amongst his subjects as a witness to events, whether with

---

[185] Hahn, 'Peregrinatio et Natio', 129–30.

Figure 20 Apotheosis of Edmund, New York, Pierpont Morgan Library,
MS M.736, fol. 22v. © The Morgan Library and Museum, New York.

a historical or a spiritual eye. In the apotheosis image, however, Edmund seems
to emerge from the space of the miniature and into the viewer's space, an effect
achieved in part by the kneeling monks who break the space of the miniature,
reaching across its border to kiss Edmund's feet, and in part by Edmund's own
wide-eyed frontal stare. The coronation and apotheosis are the only two

miniatures in the manuscript in which the viewer is confronted by a figure's frontal gaze. In both cases that gaze is meant to convey majesty and authority, but in this final image the commanding nature of the king's expression has grown exponentially, and the image is modelled on traditional representations of Christ in Majesty. This final image presents a judgemental saint, both the focus of veneration, as one would expect in a work designed to promote a saint's cult, and one to be feared, one who could return to defend the monastery and England at any time.

The miniatures are the work of the Alexis Master who is credited with founding the 'St Alban's' style, an important twelfth-century style of English illumination. The style contains elements of earlier English art, such as the expressive gestures and energetic poses of some of the figures and some of the linear detailing of the drapery, but it is most notable for its departure from the outline drawing style and from the colour washes and elaborate borders of pre-Conquest manuscripts. The colour blocks and patterns of the backgrounds and borders, elongated figures, oval faces with their wide eyes, and rich saturated colours show the influence of Ottonian and Byzantine art. The patterns of highlighting and shadow along with details such as the crown of the apotheosis miniature are taken from Byzantine art. This reminds us that England was now part of the much larger Norman Empire, and the new style was a clear expression of its international connections. It combined aspects of the northern European styles of art familiar to William the Conqueror with the styles of the Mediterranean world and his counterparts to the south, including Roger I and his successors in Sicily. The island was again part of an empire that united it with the Mediterranean world, Africa, and the Middle East, even if that empire was not as large, unified, or powerful as that of the Romans.

Kathy Lavezzo documents the English use of maps and geographical description to project an image of their self-authored exceptionalism onto the globe.[186] She begins with the Cotton world map and ends with Tudor mapmaking and ceremonial and the dawning of the age of Empire, a period in which England once again claimed the power of Rome for itself through both geographic expansion and separation from the Roman Church. This roughly half a millennium saw a continued reworking of the idea of the otherworldly island at the edge of the known world that endured well into the modern era.[187] This was not how the rest of the world viewed England, even if they did locate it on the edge. One telling image of the view of, rather than from, England is provided by the world map compiled 1140–54 by the Islamicate scholar Abu Abdallāh

---

[186] Lavezzo, *Angels on the Edge of the World*.
[187] See also Brackmann, *Elizabethan Invention*.

Muhammad ibn Muhammad ibn Abdallāh ibn Idris al-sharif al-Idrīsī (known as al-Idrīsī). The map was part of a book of the known world, the *Pleasure of him who longs to travel the world* (*Kitāb nuzhat al-mushtāq fī khtirāq al-āfāq*), illustrated with seventy regional maps and the world map. It is preserved in multiple copies made during the fourteenth century or later, with the Oxford, Bodleian Library, Pococke MS 375 copy of 1553 considered to be one of the best.[188] Reconstructions of the map are also widely available online but are sometimes mistakenly reoriented to provide a northern European perspective. Al-Idrīsī's map places south at the top and north at the bottom, projecting a view from the south out at the rest of the world. It is also concerned with the world as it was perceived and experienced by multiple peoples and from multiple perspectives, rather than one that was a projection of any one place. That does not make it any less political.

Al-Idrīsī was born in North Africa, possibly Ceuta, and studied in Cordoba, one of the greatest educational centres of the time. He had travelled widely before he arrived at Roger II's court in Palermo,[189] and England was amongst the places he visited. His book and its maps rely on earlier maps and geographies, including those of Ptolemy, Paulus Orosius, the long Islamicate tradition of geographical scholarship and mapmaking exemplified by maps produced in tenth-century Baghdad by Abū al-Qāim Muhammad ibn Hawqal, and the anonymous author of the eleventh-century manuscript known as *The Book of Curiosities of the Sciences and Marvels for the Eyes*, as well as on information from contemporary travellers and informants. It is seen as 'the first serious attempt to integrate the three classical Mediterranean traditions of Greek, Latin and Arabic scholarship in one compendium of the known world'.[190] The book is a testament to the cultural diversity and learning of Roger II's Palermo, but it is also a statement and critique of Norman imperial expansion.[191] The text praises Roger and Sicily, but it also traces the limits of Norman rule and knowledge and exalts the beauty of Rome and the authority of the pope, with whom Roger was in conflict.[192] Perhaps, like the Bayeux Embroidery or the Harley Psalter, it too allows the reader to read into the map and descriptions what they hope to find there.

Al-Idrīsī divides the world into seven longitudinal climates, following the Ptolemaic tradition, and each climate into ten sections. South is at the top of the world, in accordance with the geographies of the Balkhi school based in

[188] See https://digital.bodleian.ox.ac.uk/objects/ced0d8bd-1019-4af2-9086-e411115f1507/.

[189] Maqbul Ahmad, 'Cartography', 156; Brotton, *History of the World*, 66–7.

[190] Brotton, *History of the World*, 73.

[191] Brotton, *History of the World*, 55; Chism, 'Britain and the Sea'.

[192] Maqbul Ahmad, 'Cartography', 158; Brotton, *History of the World*, 76–7.

Baghdad.[193] The extreme south and north remain unknown and uncharted, due to their excessive heat and cold respectively. The Fortunate Isles (often identified as the Canary Islands) sit at the world's western limit and Korea at its eastern limit. England occupies sections 1 and 2 of zone 7 in the map's lower right corner. Ireland is uninhabited, so England floats quite literally on the edge of the known world. It is fragmented, with southern Scotland uninhabited and northern Scotland depicted as a separate uninhabited island, details that mark the limits of Norman rule in the north and Norman know-ledge at Roger's court in the south. The most northerly of the Anglo-Norman cities to be mapped is Durham. Wales, not yet subject to Norman rule and so not yet 'known', is absent. As Christine Chism notes, the longing and desire expressed in the title of the geography combine carnal and intellectual desire, violence and pleasure, with a world that remains ultimately beyond the grasp of any single culture, religion, or ruler.[194] It encapsulates the limits of both imperial expansion and colonial desire. Chism, following Paul Lunde, notes that England is surrounded by the *bahr muzlim* (sea of darkness or shadows), rather than the *bahr al-muhit* (encircling sea), or the *bahr al-Atlas* (sea of the Atlas mountains), all of which are names for the Atlantic Ocean. The Latin name for the Atlantic, *mare tenebrosum*, also translates as the sea of darkness; however, in the Muslim world darkness had a specific resonance with the ignorance of those outside the religion, as described in Quar'anic Surah 24, al-Nur, 'The light'.[195] Al-Idrīsī's explicit mix of knowledge and desire with the unknowable ensures that the island remains shrouded in darkness and ignorance for the Arabic reader. As Chism points out:

> If English writers describing England from within have capitalized upon geographical remoteness and parlayed it into an aura of sacralized exceptionalism ... al-Idrīsī, writing Britain from afar, uses remoteness and the darkness which it engenders to implicate the exhaustive completism of Roger II's terrestrial survey. He also suggests the futility of trans-regional Norman world-building. The view from abroad weaves the edginess of England into something far more complicated – a view of the earth itself as island whose littorals are patched together with cognition defying obfuscation.[196]

Empires, and empire-building, the map warns, will never contain that which they set out to possess.

Politically, Britannia/England was a part of a larger European world, a union of ethnicities, races, religions, and cultures, both under the Romans and under

---

[193] Maqbul Ahmad, 'Cartography', 158.   [194] Chism, 'Britain and the Sea', 503.
[195] Lunde, 'Pillars of Hercules'; Chism, 'Britain and the Sea', 507.
[196] Chism, 'Britain and the Sea', 507–9

the Normans. Between the two empires, and indeed from the civil war of the twelfth century through to the end of the Middle Ages, England struggled with maintaining a view of itself as simultaneously the exceptional island on the edge of the world and part of an international and interconnected medieval world. In the Elizabethan period, England revitalised and projected a strong sense of national identity rooted in the centuries before the coming of the Normans, one that rested on a national vision of law, language, and religion that was traced back to King Alfred and the West Saxon court.[197] Alfred and Alfredian England also occupy well-rehearsed places in modern English nationalism from the Renaissance through to Brexit.[198] But, as one recent commentator wrote, England under Boris Johnson operates on the assumption that a country can 'go global by going insular' and an empty blustering about leading the world in one thing or another,[199] an attitude that can be traced back to early medieval England and has a much broader source than Alfred and his court.

Unfortunately, there is as yet no study of the role of early medieval English art in the expansion or trappings of Empire, nationalism, and racism in the modern world. There is no scope to do such a project justice here, so I'll end with another look back at England and its relationship to the Mediterranean world, one that triangulates the southern Mediterranean worlds of Abbot Hadrian and al-Idrīsī with the England to which both had successfully travelled. This image of a ghostly English past is conveyed through the situated and complexly layered storytelling of two contemporary artists whose works and voices counter the perceived objectivity and distance of so many of the male voices of early medieval history. In Section 1 I discussed Theodore and Hadrian, two prominent immigrants from the Mediterranean world, and the enduring cultural contributions they made to seventh-century England. Hadrian was a refugee from Cerenia in what is now Libya, who fled to southern Italy during the Arab invasion of North Africa. But Hadrian's position in the church also made him an elite and exceptional figure, and there were other stories of less privileged travellers to the island that have been lost – like those of the unnamed Black skeletons identified by archaeologists. Libya, more precisely Gargash, near Tripoli, was also the launching point for a small rubber boat crammed with seventy-two refugees that set off without food or water for the Italian island of Lampedusa in March 2011. It ran out of

---

[197] See, for example, Wright, 'Dispersal of the Monastic Libraries'; Brackmann, *Elizabethan Invention*.

[198] Frantzen and Niles, *Anglo-Saxonism*; Niles, *Idea of Anglo-Saxon England*; Yorke, 'Alfredism'; Yorke, '"Old North" from the Saxon South'; Hannan, *How We Invented Freedom*, 73, 84; Ellard, *Anglo-Saxon(ist) Pasts*; Karkov, *Imagining Anglo-Saxon England*, chap. 4.

[199] McDonagh, 'Dominic Cummings Affair'.

fuel and eventually drifted back to the coast of Libya, reaching land at Zlitan. Only nine of the refugees survived. Their horrible fate was observed by NATO ships, European fishing vessels, an Italian search and rescue plane, a rescue helicopter, and other aircraft, but no one actually attempted to rescue them – a situation that continues. The tragedy was widely reported and widely censured.[200] The story of the migrant boat forms part of the poet and multimedia artist Caroline Bergvall's project *Drift*. Bergvall is an immigrant, although one from the north, an Anglo-Norwegian living in England. *Drift* exists in different but interlocking forms as a book, a series of drawings, poems, and performances. It is a compilation of texts, artworks, and archived performances that is different in medium yet also recalls other fragmentary compilations, or works that were assembled over time, like Sutton Hoo or the *Beowulf* manuscript. Bergvall uses the Old English poem *The Seafarer* (from the c.1000 compilation the Exeter Book), language, voice, music, the phenomenon of ink on paper, and a mix of narrative forms and technologies, including the story of the African migrants, to weave together a work that resists an isolated existence in either the past or the present, the there or the here. Old English morphs and mixes with modern English, and the words of travellers on the sea thread through each other, over paths that converge and diverge. Bergvall explores multiple journeys in and through English to reveal the ways in which 'the ancient cohabits with the present', with the early medieval poem about exile on the sea tracing contemporary stories of exile, migration, and loss – and vice versa. Language, sea-travel, and exile draw the voyage of the seafarer in the Old English poem into dialogue with Bergvall's own voyages and those of the African refugees in a space of timelessness and placelessness that is all about the longing for and connection to place. *Drift* allows us to see the past and the present as spaces in which each can question, comment on, and critique the other. It sets a story of privilege alongside one of hardship, a story of whose voices count and whose don't, who is able to travel safely and who is not.

In Section 3, I discussed the Sutton Hoo Mound 1 burial and its twenty-first-century reappearance in the film *The Dig*, as well as the Sutton Hoo Ship's Company project to reconstruct, or 'resurrect', the burial ship. Here, at the end, I put the Sutton Hoo ship and its resurrected ghost into dialogue with Zineb Sedira's *Floating Coffins* (Figure 21) across a time and space similar to that of *The Seafarer* and *Drift*. Sedira is also an immigrant, a Franco-Algerian artist whose personal history of migration continues *Drift*'s movement from Africa north to England. Her parents were migrants who crossed the Mediterranean in

---

[200] See, for example, BBC News, 'Nato "failed to aid"'.

Figure 21 Zenib Sedira, *Floating Coffins*. © Zineb Sedira. All Rights Reserved, DACS/Artimage 2021. Image courtesy of kamel mennour, Paris. Photo: Bartosz Kali.

a boat from Algeria to France, where Sedira was born. She subsequently migrated to London, where her own daughter was born. Her work is intensely autoethnographic and situated in the migrant/refugee experience. Her 2002 installation *Mother Tongue*, for example, deals with memory, storytelling, language, the relationship between language and identity, and the void created by incomprehensibility across the mother tongues of three generations: her mother (Arabic), herself (French), and her daughter (English).[201]

Floating Coffins (2009) is the last in a trilogy of works exploring migration and dislocation in the context of the colonial histories of France and England, with racism providing the common ground.[202] It consists of a series of films and photographs of the graveyard of over 200 rotting ships located off the Mauritanian coast, and it is accompanied by a sound-piece by the London-based, Greek-born artist Mikhail Karikis.[203] The Mauritanian harbour of Nouadhibour is an exit point for migrants from the Canary Islands attempting to reach Europe. The rotting ships are remnants of the corruption at the heart of

---

[201] See www.tate.org.uk/art/artworks/sedira-mother-tongue-t12315; https://vimeo.com /154326390. Sedira's daughter does not speak Arabic, and her mother does not speak English.

[202] The other two parts of the trilogy are *Saphir* (2006) and *MiddleSea* (2008).

[203] See www.zinebsedira.com/floating-coffins-2009/; www.tate.org.uk/art/artworks/sedira-floating-coffins-t13331.

the exchange of both goods and people between the African south and the European north, as well as the racism and hypocrisy of a Europe in which fish from African waters is coveted while migrants in search of a sustainable life are turned away.[204] Carmen Juliá has written of the work: 'This unique phenomenon on the Saharan shores represents both a hazard to shipping and an ecological threat. Also, the sea becomes a place of decline and an active wasteland where lifeless ships and human bodies can be found when rejected by the sea. Like a fishnet, the sand catches discarded goods displaced from their original home. Noxious waters and dying boats are vomiting intoxicated fishes and shattered objects.'[205]

The body in Sutton Hoo Mound 1 was carefully laid to rest in the sandy soil of East Anglia surrounded by treasure and safely enclosed in a wooden ship before the acidic soil dissolved the remains of both. They are ghosts of a medieval past that, as both the World War II years and the resurrection of the Sutton Hoo ship today show, keep coming back to haunt the present, reminding us of the fantasy of the impermeable island. Sedira's *Floating Coffins*, on the other hand, presents the very real rotting and toxic remains of ships that carried living people, many of whom died at sea and have been lost forever, their lives and journeys memorialised only by shattered objects and placeless dislocation. It confronts us with the fact that Sutton Hoo, both then and now, and the maritime history and experience it represents are not *our* heritage and represent a history and a story with which not everyone in England feels a connection, other than to their exclusion from it. Not everyone in England today has a heritage that involves coming safely to shore or treasure-filled royal burial grounds, but everyone in England today has a transoceanic heritage somewhere in the past.

The medieval and the modern cannot and should not be separated from each other into discrete periods, one safely tucked away in an objectified and distant past, the other an equally objectified and distant academic space from which we look back. Such a view prevents us from confronting the problems created by the periodisation and disciplinary definitions that separate the histories and experiences of the many different cultural, ethnic, and racial identities of the people who made the journey to Britain/England from the early medieval period to the present day. To put *Floating Coffins* side by side with the Sutton Hoo ship creates a potent art-historical reminder of the wreckage of imperial expansion and colonial desire charted by al-Idrīsī and lying dormant within the Cotton world map.

---

[204] Gogarty, 'Zineb Sedira'.   [205] Juliá, 'Floating Coffins'.

Abbreviations

B.L.	British Library
C.A.S.S.S.	Corpus of Anglo-Saxon Stone Sculpture
C.C.C.C.	Cambridge, Corpus Christi College

Bibliography

Primary

Ælfric, Abbot of Eynsham. (1991) *Colloquy*, edited by George Norman Garmonsway, new ed. Exeter: Exeter University Press.

Barlow, Frank. (1992) *The Life of King Edward who Rests at Westminster, Attributed to a Monk of Saint-Bertin*, 2nd ed. Oxford: Oxford University Press.

Barney, Stephen A., et al., ed. and trans. (2006) *The Etymologies of Isidore of Seville*. Cambridge: Cambridge University Press.

Campbell, Alistair, ed. (1967) *De Abbatibus*. Oxford: Oxford University Press.

Colgrave, Bertram, ed. and trans. (1927) *The Life of Bishop Wilfrid by Eddius Stephanus*. Cambridge: Cambridge University Press.

Corpus of Anglo-Saxon Stone Sculpture. www.ascorpus.ac.uk.

Dictionary of Old English. https://tapor-library-utoronto-ca.eu1.proxy.openathens.net/doe/.

Gates, Jay. (2018) 'Prologue to the Laws of King Alfred: An Edition and Translation for Students'. *Heroic Age* 18. www.heroicage.org/issues/18/gates.php.

Godden, Malcolm R., ed. (2016) *Old English History of the World: An Anglo-Saxon Rewriting of Orosius*. Cambridge, MA: Harvard University Press.

Godden, Malcolm, and Susan Irvine, eds. (2009) *The Old English Boethius: An Edition of the Old English Version of Boethius's De Consolatione Philosophiae*, 2 vols. Oxford: Oxford University Press.

Gregory the Great. (1971) *Homiliae in Hiezechihelem*, edited by M. Adriaen. CCSL 142. Turnhout: Brepols.

Jones, Christopher A., ed. and trans. (2012) *Old English Shorter Poems*, vol. 1, *Religious and Didactic*. Cambridge, MA: Harvard University Press.

Muir, Bernard, ed. (1994) *The Exeter Anthology of Old English Poetry: An Edition of Exeter Dean and Chapter MS 3501*. Exeter: Exeter University Press.

Winterbottom, Michael, ed. and trans. (1978) *Gildas. The Ruin of Britain and Other Documents*. Arthurian Period Sources, vol. 7. London: Phillimore.

Wright, David H. (1967) *The Vespasian Psalter*, Early English Manuscripts in Facsimile 14. Copenhagen: Rosenkilde and Bagger.

Secondary

Abou-el-Haj, Barbara. (1983) 'Bury St Edmunds Abbey between 1070 and 1124: A History of Property, Privilege and Monastic Art Production'. *Art History* 6: 1–30.

Adams, Noël. (2010) 'Rethinking the Sutton Hoo Shoulder Clasps'. In *'Intelligible Beauty': Recent Research on Byzantine Jewellery*, edited by Chris Entwhistle and Noël Adams, pp. 83–112. London: British Museum Press.

Addley, Esther. (2019) '"One of the Greatest Finds": Experts Shed Light on Staffordshire Hoard'. *The Guardian*, 1 November 2019. www.theguardian .com/culture/2019/nov/01/staffordshire-hoard-archaeologists-academic-research-gold-ornaments.

Alberge, Dalya. (2020) 'Hadrian's Wall Dig Reveals Oldest Christian Graffiti on Chalice'. *The Guardian*, 29 August 2020. www.theguardian.com/uk-news/2020/aug/29/hadrians-wall-dig-reveals-oldest-christian-graffiti-on-chalice.

Allfrey, Francesca. (2020) 'Sutton Hoo in Public: Newspapers, Television, and Museums'. Unpub. PhD Thesis, King's College London.

Ashe, Laura, and Emily Joan Ward, eds. (2020) *Conquests in Eleventh Century England: 1016, 1066*. Woodbridge, UK: Boydell & Brewer.

Bailey, Richard N. (2010) *Corpus of Anglo-Saxon Stone Sculpture 9, Cheshire and Lancashire*. Oxford: Oxford University Press.

Bailey, Richard N., and Rosemary Cramp. (1988) *Corpus of Anglo-Saxon Stone Sculpture 2, Cumberland, Westmorland and Lancashire North-of-the-Sands*. Oxford: Oxford University Press.

Barker, Philip, et al. (1997) *The Baths-Basilica Wroxeter: Excavations 1966–90*. London: English Heritage.

BBC News. (2012) 'Nato "failed to aid" Libyan Migrant Boat – Council of Europe Report'. 29 March 2012. www.bbc.co.uk/news/world-europe-17548410.

Benítez-Rojo, Antonio. (1992) *The Repeating Island*, trans. James E. Mariniss. Durham, NC: Duke University Press.

Bidwell, Paul. (2010) 'A Survey of the Anglo-Saxon Crypt at Hexham and its Reused Roman Stonework'. *Archaeologia Aeliana* 5th ser. 39: 53–145.

Bischoff, Bernhard, and Michael Lapidge. (1994) *Biblical Commentaries from the Canterbury School of Theodore and Hadrian*. Cambridge: Cambridge University Press.

Bitterli, Dieter. (2009) *Say What I am Called: The Old English Riddles of the Exeter Book and the Anglo-Latin Riddle Tradition*. Toronto: University of Toronto Press.

Blurton, Heather. (2008) '*Reliquia*: Writing Relics in Anglo-Norman Durham'. In *Cultural Diversity in the British Middle Ages: Archipelago, Island, England*, edited by Jeffrey Jerome Cohen, pp. 39–56. New York: Palgrave.

Brackmann, Rebecca. (2012) *The Elizabethan Invention of Anglo-Saxon England: Laurence Nowell, William Lambarde and the Study of Old English*. Cambridge: D. S. Brewer.

Breay, Claire, and Joanna Story, eds. (2018) *Anglo-Saxon Kingdoms: Art, Word, War*. London: British Library.

Brooks, Nicholas. (1991) 'Historical Introduction'. In *The Making of England: Anglo-Saxon Art and Culture AD 600–900*, edited by Leslie Webster and Janet Backhouse, pp. 9–14. London: The British Museum Press.

Brotton, Jerry. (2012) *A History of the World in Twelve Maps*. London: Penguin.

Brown, Michelle P. (2001) 'Female Book-Ownership and Production in Anglo-Saxon England: The Evidence of the Prayerbooks'. In *Lexis and Texts in Early English: Studies Presented to Jane Roberts*, edited by Christian J. Kay and Louise M. Sylvester, pp. 45–67. Amsterdam: Rodopi.

(2001) 'Mercian Manuscripts? The "Tiberius" Group and its Historical Context'. In *Mercia: An Anglo-Saxon Kingdom in Europe*, edited by Michelle P. Brown and Carol A. Farr, pp. 278–91. Leicester: Leicester University Press.

(2003) *The Lindisfarne Gospels: Society, Spirituality and the Scribe*. London: British Library.

Brunning, Sue. (2019) *The Sword in Early Medieval Northern Europe: Experience, Identity, Representation*. Woodbridge, UK: Boydell & Brewer.

Budny, Mildred, and Dominic Tweddle. (1984) 'The Maaseik Embroideries'. *Anglo-Saxon England*, 13: 65–96.

Cameron, Neil. (1994) 'The Romanesque Sculpture of Dunfermline Abbey: Durham versus the Vicinal'. In *Medieval Art and Architecture in the Diocese of St Andrews*, edited by John Higgitt, British Archaeological Association Conference Transactions 14, pp. 118–23. London: Routledge.

Caviness, Madeline H. (2001) 'Anglo-Saxon Women, Norman Knights and a "Third Sex". In the Bayeux Embroidery', *Reframing Medieval Art: Difference, Margins, Boundaries*, ch. 2. http://dca.lib.tufts.edu/caviness/chapter2.html.

Chazelle, Celia. (2004) 'Violence and the Virtuous Ruler in the Utrecht Psalter'. In *The Illustrated Psalter: Studies in the Content, Purpose, and Placement of its Images*, edited by Friedrich Otto Büttner, pp. 311–26. Turnhout: Brepols.

Chism, Christine. (2016) 'Britain and the Sea of Darkness: Islandology in al-Idrīsī's *Nuzhat al-Mushtaq*'. *postmedieval: A Journal of Medieval Cultural Studies* 7: 497–510.

Coatsworth, Elizabeth. (2008) *Corpus of Anglo-Saxon Stone Sculpture 8, Western Yorkshire*. Oxford: Oxford University Press.

Coatsworth, Elizabeth, and Michael Pinder. (2012) *Art of the Anglo-Saxon Goldsmith: Fine Metalwork in Anglo-Saxon England: Its Practice and Practitioners*. Woodbridge, UK: Boydell & Brewer.

Daniels, Robin. (1988) 'The Anglo-Saxon Monastery at Church Close, Hartlepool, Cleveland'. *Archaeological Journal* 145: 158–210.

D'Arcens, Louise. (2021) 'The Dig's Romanticisation of an Anglo-Saxon Past Reveals It Is a Film for Post-Brexit UK'. *The Conversation*, 15 February 2021. https://theconversation.com/the-digs-romanticisation-of-an-anglo-saxon-past-reveals-it-is-a-film-for-post-brexit-uk-154827?fbclid=IwAR1-1T0JUTZ2Q4Lx8xdYkOH7XTj-N0jm24AaPGFuzvq2PPovpstzGQUV2H0.

Davies, Robert Rees (2000) *The First English Empire: Power and Identities in the British Isles 1093–1343*. Oxford: Oxford University Press.

DeLoughrey, Elizabeth M. (2007) *Routes and Roots: Navigating Caribbean and Pacific Island Literatures*. Honolulu: University of Hawaii Press.

Deshman, Robert. (1995) *The Benedictional of Æthelwold*. Princeton, NJ: Princeton University Press.

Discenza, Nicole Guenther. (2001) 'Alfred's Verse Preface to the *Pastoral Care* and the Chain of Authority'. *Neophilologus* 85: 625–33.

Dodwell, Charles Reginald (1982) *Anglo-Saxon Art: A New Perspective*. Ithaca, NY: Cornell University Press.

Drauschke, Jörg. (2010) 'Byzantine Jewellery? Amethyst Beads in East and West during the Early Byzantine Period'. In *'Intelligible Beauty': Recent Research on Byzantine Jewellery*, edited by Chris Entwhistle and Noël Adams, pp. 50–60. London: British Museum Press.

Ellard, Donna Beth. (2019) *Anglo-Saxon(ist) Pasts postSaxon Futures*. Earth, Milky Way: punctum books.

Fairweather, Janet, trans. (2005) *Liber Eliensis: A History of the Isle of Ely from the Seventh Century to the Twelfth*. Woodbridge, UK: Boydell &|Brewer.

Fawcett, Richard. (2005) 'Dunfermline Abbey Church'. In *Royal Dunfermline*, edited by Richard Fawcett, pp. 27–63. Edinburgh: Society of Antiquaries of Scotland.

Fern, Chris, et al. (2019) *The Staffordshire Hoard: An Anglo-Saxon Treasure*. London: Society of Antiquaries.

Fernie, Eric. (1994) 'The Romanesque Churches of Dunfermline Abbey'. In *Medieval Art and Architecture in the Diocese of St Andrews*, edited by John Higgitt, British Archaeological Association Conference Transactions 14, pp. 25–37. London: Routledge.

Fleming, Damian. (2004) 'Eþel-Weard: The First Scribe in the Beowulf MS'. *Neuphilologische Mitteilungen: Bulletin de La Société Néophilologique/ Bulletin of the Modern Language Society* 105: 177–86.

Foys, Martin, Heather Wacha, et al. (2020) 'Morgenwergas (Cotton Map, BL Cotton Tiberius Bv, f. 56v)'. *Virtual Mappa*. Schoenberg Institute of Manuscript Studies.nstitute of Manuscript Studies:hapter (Section) 1 of this work? for this bookto be sure the numbering i s at all for anything, https://sims2.digitalmappa.org/36.

Frantzen, Allen J., and John D. Niles, eds. (1997) *Anglo-Saxonism and the Construction of Social Identity.* Gainesville: University of Florida Press.

Gameson, Richard. (1990) 'The Anglo-Saxon Artists of the Harley (603) Psalter'. *Journal of the British Archaeological Association* 143: 29–48.

  (2011) 'An Itinerant English Master around the Millennium'. In *England and the Continent in the Tenth Century: Studies in Honour of Wilhelm Levison (1876–1947)*, edited by David Rollason, Conrad Leyser, and Howard Williams, pp. 87–134. Turnhout: Brepols.

Gerrard, James. (2013) *The Ruin of Britain: An Archaeological Perspective.* Cambridge: Cambridge University Press.

Gogarty, Larne Abse. (2009) 'Zineb Sedira: Current of Time'. *Art Monthly* 328: 34.

Gowland, Rebecca. (2017) 'Embodied Identities in Roman Britain: A Bioarchaeological Approach'. *Britannia* 48: 177–94.

Gransden, Antonia, ed. (1998) *Bury St. Edmunds Medieval Art, Architecture, Archaeology and Economy.* London: Routledge.

Green, Caitlin R. (2016) 'A Note on the Evidence for African Migrants in Britain from the Bronze Age to the Medieval Period'. www.caitlingreen .org/2016/05/a-note-on-evidence-for-african-migrants.html.

  (2016) 'Indo-Pacific Beads from Europe to Japan? Another Fifth- to Seventh-Century AD Global Distribution'. www.caitlingreen.org/2018/07/indo-pacific-beads-europe.html?fbclid=IwAR1qEQj-JUszSPd26hoRO EDyDa6Vh5rOr5qQfSKRdpGQJv_VonOQA67hbQo.

Hadley, Dawn M. (2020) 'The Archaeology of Migrants in Viking Age and Anglo-Norman England: Process, Practice, and Performance'. In *Migrants in Medieval England c.500–c.1500*, edited by W. Mark Ormrod, Joanna Story, and Elizabeth M. Tyler, pp. 175–205. Oxford: Oxford University Press.

Hahn, Cynthia. (1991) 'Peregrinatio et Natio: The Illustrated Life of Edmund, King and Martyr'. *Gesta* 30.2: 119–39.

Hannan, Daniel. (2013) *How We Invented Freedom and Why it Matters.* London: Head of Zeus.

Heslop, Thomas Alexander (2008) 'The Implication of the Utrecht Psalter in English Romanesque Art'. In *Romanesque Art and Thought in the Twelfth Century: Essays in Honour of Walter Cahn*, edited by Colum Hourihane, pp. 267–89. Princeton, NJ: Princeton University Press.

Hewitt, Virginia. 'Britannia (fl. 1st–21st cent.)'. *Oxford Dictionary of National Biography*. www.oxforddnb.com/view/10.1093/ref:odnb/9780198 614128.001.0001/odnb-9780198614128-e-68196;jsessionid=9956DB FDC19765547ACE34065A3089E6.

Hills, Catherine. (2017) 'From Isidore to Isotopes: Ivory Rings in Early Medieval Graves'. In *Image and Power in the Archaeology of Early Medieval Britain: Essays in Honour of Rosemary Cramp*, edited by Helena Hamerow and Arthur MacGregor, pp. 131–46. Oxford: Oxbow Books.

Hines, John. (2021) 'What is the Future of the Past', *Current Archaeology*. www.archaeology.co.uk/articles/what-is-the-future-of-the-past.htm.

Holcomb, Melanie. (2009) 'Strokes of Genius: The Draftsman's Art in the Middle Ages'. In *Pen and Parchment: Drawing in the Middle Ages*. New York: Metropolitan Museum of Art.

Housley, Marjorie. (2020) 'Uneasy Presences: Revulsion and the Necropolitics of Attachment'. *postmedieval: A Journal of Medieval Cultural Studies* 11.4: 434–41.

Huggett, Jeremy. (1988) 'Imported Grave Goods and the Early Anglo-Saxon Economy'. *Medieval Archaeology* 32.1: 63–96.

Irvine, Susan. (2015) 'The Alfredian Prefaces and Epilogues'. In *A Companion to Alfred the Great*, edited by Nicole Guenther Discenza and Paul E. Szarmach, pp. 143–70. Leiden: Brill.

Johnson-South, Ted. (2001) *Historia de Sancto Cuthberto: A History of Saint Cuthbert and a Record of his Patrimony*. Cambridge: D. S. Brewer.

Jones, Chris. (2019) 'Relining *The Grave*: A Slow Reading of MS Bodley 343, fol. 170r'. In *Slow Scholarship: Medieval Research and the Neoliberal University*, edited by Catherine E. Karkov, pp. 52–77. Cambridge: D. S. Brewer.

Juliá, Carmen. (2009) 'Floating Coffins 2009: Summary'. www.tate.org.uk/art/ artworks/sedira-floating-coffins-t13331.

Karkov, Catherine E. (2006) 'Writing and Having Written: Word and Image in the Eadwig Gospels'. In *Writing and Texts in Anglo-Saxon England*, edited by Alexander R. Rumble, pp. 44–61. Woodbridge, UK: Boydell & Brewer.

(2011) *The Art of Anglo-Saxon England*. Woodbridge, UK: Boydell & Brewer.

(2012) 'Postcolonial'. In *A Handbook of Anglo-Saxon Studies*, edited by Jacqueline Stodnick and Renée Trilling, pp. 149–63. Chichester: Wiley Blackwell.

(2017) 'Reading the Trinity in the Harley Psalter'. In *Crossing Boundaries: Interdisciplinary Approaches to the Art, Material Culture, Language and Literature of the Early Medieval World*, edited by Jane Hawkes and Eric Cambridge, pp. 90–6. Oxford: Oxbow Books.

(2020) 'Conquest and Material Culture'. In *Conquests in Eleventh Century England: 1016, 1066*, edited by Laura Ashe and Emily Joan Ward, pp. 183–205. Woodbridge, UK: Boydell & Brewer.

(2020) *Imagining Anglo-Saxon England: Utopia, Heterotopia, Dystopia*. Woodbridge, UK: Boydell & Brewer.

(Forthcoming) 'Alternative Histories: Phantom Truths in Stone'. In *Vera Lex Historiae: Constructing Truth in Medieval Historical Narrative Traditions*, edited by Michael Kelley and Catalin Taranu. Binghamton, NY: Gracchi.

Karkov, Catherine E., and Elaine Treharne. (Forthcoming, 2022) 'The Presence of the Hands: Sculpture and Script in the Eighth to Twelfth Centuries'. In *Medieval English and Dutch Literatures: The European Context, Essays in Honor of David F. Johnson*, edited by Larissa Tracy and Geert Claassens. Woodbridge, UK: Boydell & Brewer

Kay, Sarah. (2020) 'Siren Enchantments, or, Reading Sound in Medieval Books'. *SubStance* 49.2: 108–32.

Kempshall, Matthew. (2001) 'No Bishop, No King: The Ministerial Ideology of Kingship and Asser's *Res Gestae Aelfredi*'. In *Belief and Culture in the Middle Ages*, edited by Richard Gameson and Henrietta Leyser, pp. 106–27. Oxford: Oxford University Press.

Kim, Susan M. (2005) '"As I Once Did with Grendel": Boasting and Nostalgia in *Beowulf*'. *Modern Philology* 103.1: 4–27.

Klukas, Arnold William (1983/4) 'The Architectural Implications of the *Decreta Lanfranci*'. *Anglo-Norman Studies* 6: 136–71.

Lavezzo, Kathy. (2006) *Angels on the Edge of the World: Geography, Literature, and English Community 1000–1534*. Ithaca, NY: Cornell University Press.

Lunde, Paul. (1992) 'Pillars of Hercules, Sea of Darkness'. *Aramco World: The Middle East and the Age of Discovery* 43.3. https://archive.aramcoworld.com/issue/199203/pillars.of.hercules.sea.of.darkness.htm.

MacGregor, Arthur. (1985) *Bone, Antler, Ivory and Horn: The Technology of Skeletal Materials Since the Roman Period*. London: Barnes & Noble.

Manion, Mags. (2017) 'Symbolism, Performance and Colour: The Use of Glass Beads in Early Medieval Ireland'. In *Islands in a Global Context: Proceedings of the Seventh International Conference on Insular Art*, edited by Conor Newman, Mags Manion, and Fiona Gavin, pp. 149–58. Dublin: Four Courts Press.

Maqbul Ahmad, Sayyid. (1992) 'Cartography of al-Sharīf al-Idrīsī'. In *The History of Cartography*, edited by J. B. Harley and David Woodward, vol. 2, book 1, *Cartography in the Traditional Islamic and South Asian Societies*, pp. 156–72. Chicago, IL: University of Chicago Press.

McColl, Alan. (2006) 'The Meaning of "Britain" in Medieval and Early Modern England'. *Journal of British Studies* 45: 248–69.

McDonagh, Bobby. (2020) 'Dominic Cummings Affair Reflects Brexit Exceptionalism'. *Irish Times*, 25 May 2020. www.irishtimes.com/opin ion/dominic-cummings-affair-reflects-brexit-exceptionalism-1.4261255? fbclid=IwAR2XZS1T3XfMjJlg3r6mrFvbaOUkmrWD0uP-CWdNU4n N3JifC7PPBMTOsDc#.Xsy_C5Y_NKE.facebook.

McGuigan, Neil. (2015) 'Neither Scotland nor England: Middle Britain c. 850–1150'. Unpublished PhD dissertation, University of St Andrews.

Mittman, Asa Simon, and Susan M. Kim. (2013) *Inconceivable Beasts: The Wonders of the East in the Beowulf Manuscript*. Tempe, AZ: ACMRS.

Mittman, Asa Simon, and Patricia MacCormack. (2016) 'Rebuilding the Fabulated Bodies of the Hoard-Warriors'. *postmedieval: a journal of medieval cultural studies* 7.3: 356–68.

Miyashiro, Adam. (2020) 'Homeland Insecurity: Biopolitics and Sovereign Violence in *Beowulf*'. *postmedieval: a journal of medieval cultural studies* 11.4: 384–95.

Montgomery Ramírez, Paul Edward. 'Colonial Representation of Race in Alternative Museums: The "African" of St Benet's, the "Arab" of Jorvik, and the Black Viking'. *International Journal of Heritage Studies* (2021): 1–16. DOI: 10.1080/13527258.2021.1883715.

Morris, Stefan. (2020) 'Stunning Dark Age Mosaic Found at Roman Villa in Cotswolds'. *The Guardian*, 10 December 2020. www.theguardian.com/uk-news/2020/dec/10/stunning-dark-ages-mosaic-found-atroman-villa-in-cots wolds?fbclid=IwAR32toRe3jOk0zNb9ghdugn_YCqKJDzJAePuBLToM nw2_Hds1mlydJT9m4.

Naismith, Rory. https://twitter.com/rory_naismith/status/97314602773 6825856?lang=en.

Nees, Lawrence. (2003) 'Reading Aldred's Colophon for the Lindisfarne Gospels'. *Speculum* 78: 333–77.

Niles, John D. (2015) *The Idea of Anglo-Saxon England 1066–1901: Remembering Forgetting, Deciphering, and Renewing the Past*. Chichester: Wiley.

Noel, William. (1995) *The Harley Psalter*. Cambridge: Cambridge University Press.

Ó Carragáin, Éamonn. (2005) *Ritual and the Rood: Liturgical Images and the Old English Poems of the Dream of the Rood Tradition*. London: British Library.

Oosthuizen, Susan. (2019) *The Emergence of the English*. Leeds: Arc Humanities Press.

Orton, Fred, and Ian Wood with Clare A. Lees. (2007) *Fragments of History: Rethinking the Ruthwell and Bewcastle Monuments*. Manchester: Manchester University Press.

Owen-Crocker, Gale R. (2010) *Dress in Anglo-Saxon England*, rev. ed. Woodbridge, UK: Boydell & Brewer.

Paz, James. (2017) *Nonhuman Voices in Anglo-Saxon Literature and Material Culture*. Manchester: Manchester University Press.

Pestell, Tim. (2018) 'These Burial Treasures Open a Window into Early Anglo-Saxon East Anglia'. https://museumcrush.org/these-burial-treasures-open-a-window-into-early-anglo-saxon-east-anglia/.

Pfaff, Richard W. (1992) 'Eadui Basan: Scriptorum Princeps?' In *England in the Eleventh Century: Proceedings of the 1990 Harlaxton Symposium*, edited by Carola Hicks, pp. 267–83. Stamford, UK: Paul Watkins, 1992.

Rambaran-Olm, Mary. (Forthcoming) 'A Wrinkle in Medieval Time: Ironing out the Problems of Periodization, Gatekeeping, and Exclusion in Early English Studies'. *New Literary History* 53.2.

Rambaran-Olm, Mary, M. Breann Leake, and Micah James Goodrich. (2020) 'Medieval Studies: The Stakes of the Field'. *postmedieval: a journal of medieval cultural studies* 11.4: 356–70.

Rambaran-Olm, Mary, and Erik Wade. (Forthcoming) *Race in Early Medieval England* Cambridge: Cambridge University Press.

Raw, Barbara. (1997) *Trinity and Incarnation in Anglo-Saxon Art and Thought*. Cambridge: Cambridge University Press.

Riddler, Ian. (2014) 'The Archaeology of the Anglo-Saxon Whale'. In *The Maritime World of the Anglo-Saxons*, edited by Stacy S. Klein, William Schipper, and Shannon Lewis-Simpson, pp. 337–54. Tempe, AZ: ACMRS.

Roberts, Jane. (2006) 'Aldred Signs Off from Glossing the Lindisfarne Gospels'. In *Writing and Texts in Anglo-Saxon England*, edited by Alexander R. Rumble, pp. 28–43. Woodbridge, UK: Boydell & Brewer.

Sauer, Michelle M. (2016). https://soundstudiesblog.com/2016/10/17/audiotac
tility-the-medieval-soundscape-of-parchment/.

Schreiber, Carolin. (2002) *King Alfred's Old English Translation of Pope
Gregory the Great's Regula Pastoralis and its Cultural Context*. Munich:
Peter Lang, 2002.

Story, Joanna, W. Mark Ormrod, and Elizabeth M. Tyler. (2020) 'Framing
Migration in Medieval England'. In *Migration in Medieval England
c. 500– c. 1500*, edited by W. Mark Ormrod, Joanna Story, and Elizabeth
M. Tyler, pp. 1–17. Oxford: Oxford University Press.

Thurlby, Malcolm. (1994) 'The Roles of the Patron and the Master Mason in the
First Design of the Romanesque Cathedral of Durham'. In *Anglo-Norman
Durham*, edited by David Rollason, Margaret Harvey, and
Michael Prestwich, pp. 161–84. Woodbridge, UK: Boydell & Brewer.

Treharne, Elaine. (2012) *Living Through Conquest: The Politics of Early
English 1020–1220*. Oxford: Oxford University Press.

Waxenberger, Gaby. (2011) 'The Cryptic Runes on the Auzon/Franks Casket:
A Challenge for the Runologist and Lexicographer'. In *More than Words:
English Lexicography and Lexicology Past and Present: Essays Presented
to Hans Sauer on the Occasion of his 65th Birthday – Part 1*, pp. 161–70.
Frankfurt am Main: Peter Lang.

(2017) 'Date and Provenance of the Auzon or Franks Casket'. In *Life on the
Edge: Social, Political and Religious Frontiers in Early Medieval Europe*,
edited by Sarah Semple, Celia Orsini, and Sean Mui, pp. 121–33. Neue
Studien zur Sachsenforschung Band 6. Braunschwieg: Braunsch
weigisches Landesmuseum.

Webster, Leslie. (2003) 'Aedficia Nova: Treasures of Alfred's Reign'. In *Alfred
the Great*, edited by Timothy Reuter, pp. 79–103. Aldershot: Ashgate.

(2010) *The Franks Casket*. London: British Museum Press.

(2012) *Anglo-Saxon Art*. London: British Museum Press.

Webster, Leslie, and Janet Backhouse, eds. (1991) *The Making of England:
Anglo-Saxon Art and Culture AD 600–900*. London: British Museum
Press.

Williams, Gareth, and Barry Ager. (2010) *The Vale of York Hoard*. London:
British Museum Press.

Williams, Howard. (2015) 'Hogbacks and the Materiality of Solid Spaces'. In
Early Medieval Stone Monuments: Materiality, Biography, Landscape,
edited by Howard Williams, Joanne Kirton, and Megan Gondek, pp.
241–68. Woodbridge, UK: Boydell & Brewer.

(2020) 'The Fight for Anglo-Saxon'. https://aeon.co/essays/why-we-should-
keep-the-term-anglo-saxon-in-archaeology.

Wilmott, Tony. (1997) *Birdoswald: Excavations of a Roman Fort on Hadrian's Wall and Its Successor Settlements: 1987–1992*. London: Historic England.

Wolfe, Patrick. (2006) 'Settler Colonialism and the Elimination of the Native'. *Journal of Genocide Research* 8.4: 387–409.

Wormald, Francis. (1952) *English Drawings of the Tenth and Eleventh Centuries*. London: Faber & Faber.

Wright, C. E. (1951) 'The Dispersal of the Monastic Libraries and the Beginning of Anglo-Saxon Studies: Matthew Parker and His Circle: A Preliminary Study'. *Transactions of the Cambridge Bibliographic Society* 1.3: 208–37.

Wright, Michael, and Kathleen Loncar, trans. (2004) 'The Vita of Edith'. In *Writing the Wilton Women`: Goscelin's Legend of Edith and Liber Confortatorius*, edited by Stephanie Hollis et al., pp. 17–93. Turnhout: Brepols.

Yorke, Barbara. (2003) 'Alfredism: The Use and Abuse of King Alfred's Reputation in Later Centuries'. In *Alfred the Great: Papers from the Eleventh-Centenary Conference*, edited by Timothy Reuter, pp. 361–80. Aldershot: Routledge.

(2009) 'The "Old North" from the Saxon South in Nineteenth-Century Britain'. In *Anglo-Saxons and the North*, edited by Matti Kilpio et al., pp. 132–49. Tempe, AZ: ACMRS.

Acknowledgements

I would like to thank the editors Megan Cavell, Rory Naismith, Emily Thornbury, and Winfried Rudolph for inviting me to write this Element, Megan and Emily for their comments and editorial assistance, and Megan in particular for her help in cutting the manuscript down to size. I would also like to thank Mary Rambaran-Olm and Erik Wade for their invaluable advice, comments, and wonderful conversations about its contents. My colleague Eva Frojmovic and the students in our Racist Pasts/Radical Futures module (their names too many to list here) were helpful critics of some of my ideas early on. The students in my Origins of Postcolonial England helped me to clarify ideas at the end. Thanks to George Beckett, Harriet Broadbent, Jack Emptage, Gaiane Jauvet, Ashleigh Jerman, Emma Kolibas, Anthony McMullin, Sofia Moore, Samuel Read, Zhuo Yang, and Jenny Williams. The anonymous peer reviewers saved me from numerous errors, and any that remain are, of course, my own. And, as always, I could not have written anything without the assistance of Boris and Natasha.

Cambridge Elements ☰

England in the Early Medieval World

Megan Cavell

University of Birmingham

Megan Cavell is a Birmingham Fellow in medieval English literature at the University of Birmingham. She works on a wide range of topics in medieval literary studies, from Old and early Middle English and Latin languages and literature to gender, material culture and animal studies. Her previous publications include *Weaving Words and Binding Bodies: The Poetics of Human Experience in Old English Literature* (2016), and she is co-editor of *Riddles at Work in the Anglo-Saxon Tradition: Words, Ideas, Interactions* with Jennifer Neville (2020).

Rory Naismith

University of Cambridge

Rory Naismith is Lecturer in the History of England Before the Norman Conquest in the Department of Anglo-Saxon, Norse and Celtic at the University of Cambridge and a Fellow of Corpus Christi College, Cambridge. Also a Fellow of the Royal Historical Society, he is the author of *Citadel of the Saxons: The Rise of Early London* (2018), *Medieval European Coinage, with a Catalogue of the Coins in the Fitzwilliam Museum, Cambridge, 8: Britain and Ireland c. 400–1066* (2017) and *Money and Power in Anglo-Saxon England: The Southern English Kingdoms 757–865* (2012, which won the 2013 International Society of Anglo-Saxonists First Book Prize).

Winfried Rudolf

University of Göttingen

Winfried Rudolf is Chair of Medieval English Language and Literature in the University of Göttingen (Germany). Recent publications include *Childhood and Adolescence in Anglo-Saxon Literary Culture* with Susan E. Irvine (2018). He has published widely on Anglo-Saxon homiletic literature and is currently principal investigator of the ERC-Project ECHOE–Electronic Corpus of Anonymous Homilies in Old English.

Emily V. Thornbury

Yale University

Emily V. Thornbury is Associate Professor of English at Yale University. She studies the literature and art of early England, with a particular emphasis on English and Latin poetry. Her publications include *Becoming a Poet in Anglo-Saxon England* (2014) and, co-edited with Rebecca Stephenson, *Latinity and Identity in Anglo-Saxon Literature* (2016). She is currently working on a monograph called *The Virtue of Ornament*, about Anglo-Saxon theories of aesthetic value.

About the Series

Elements in England in the Early Medieval World takes an innovative, interdisciplinary view of the culture, history, literature, archaeology and legacy of England between the fifth and eleventh centuries. Individual contributions question and situate key themes, and thereby bring new perspectives on the heritage of Anglo-Saxon England. They draw on texts in Latin and Old English as well as material culture to paint a vivid picture of the period. Relevant not only to students and scholars working in medieval studies, these volumes explore the rich intellectual, methodological and comparative value that the dynamic researchers interested in the Anglo-Saxon World have to offer in a modern, global context. The series is driven by a commitment to inclusive and critical scholarship, and to the view that Anglo-Saxon studies have a part to play in many fields of academic research, as well as constituting a vibrant and self-contained area of research in its own right.

Cambridge Elements ☰

England in the Early Medieval World

Printed in the United States
by Baker & Taylor Publisher Services